Praise for

THE NEW SUCCESSFUL
LARGE ACCOUNT MANAGEMENT

O9-BUB-222

"The Large Account Management Process has implemented a discipline that allows people to work together and communicate, setting strategies and sales goals that benefit both our customers and our own company."

—Joseph L. Cash, senior vice president of sales,
Equifax Corporation

"LAMP provides a methodology that enables Price Waterhouse to be viewed by our major accounts as a joint venture partner. It allows us to identify and manage client needs more effectively."

—Tom Beyer, vice chairman, management consulting
services, Price Waterhouse

"After over two and a half decades of utilizing Miller-Heiman's Strategic Selling Program, LAMP is the next logical step for Siemens Building Technologies to implement across its organization. LAMP is a valid process that helps us identify those high-impact 'Organizational Needs' and solutions that our Clients have come to expect and respect."

—Bill Clement, director, Enterprise Process
Development, Siemens Building Technologies

"Miller Heiman's Large Account Management Process delivers a disciplined process for gathering the information required to really understand the trends impacting our largest clients. This critical information defines the strategies that provide long-term customer value and drive consistently superior business results."

—Paul Wichman, vice president and senior division
sales manager, Schwab Institutional

THE NEW SUCCESSFUL LARGE ACCOUNT MANAGEMENT

Maintaining and Growing Your Most Important Assets— Your Customers

ROBERT B. MILLER
AND STEPHEN E. HEIMAN
WITH Tad Tuleja

WARNER
BUSINESS
BOOKS™

NEW YORK   BOSTON

Strategic Selling®, *Conceptual Selling*®, *LAMP*®, *Tactical Telesales*®, *Miller Heiman, Inc.*® and Logo, *Large Account Management Process*ˢᴹ, *Manager's Coaching*ˢᴹ, *Channel Partner Management*ˢᴹ, *Negotiate Success*ˢᴹ, *Selling Fundamentals*ˢᴹ, *Predictive Sales Performance Solutions*ˢᴹ, *Red Flags*ˢᴹ (words and Logo), and **MILLER HEIMAN**ˢᴹ are registered tradmarks and service marks of Miller Heiman, Inc.

Warner Business Books
Warner Books

Time Warner Book Group
1271 Avenue of the Americas, New York, NY 10020
Visit our Web site at www.twbookmark.com.

The Warner Business Books logo is a trademark of Warner Books.

Printed in the United States of America

First Warner Books Edition: May 1992
Revised and Updated: April 2005

10   9   8   7   6   5   4   3   2

Library of Congress Cataloging-in-Publication Data

Miller, Robert B. (Robert Bruce)
    The new successful large account management : maintaining and growing your most important assets—your customers / Robert B. Miller and Stephen E. Heiman, with Tad Tuleja.—Rev. and updated
        p.   cm.
    Includes index.
    ISBN 0-446-69466-5
    1. Selling—Key accounts.   2. Market segmentation.
    3. Marketing—Key accounts.   I. Heiman, Stephen E.
    II. Tuleja, Tad, 1944–   III. Title.

HF5438.8.K48M55   2005
658.8'102—dc22
                                2004023694

Book design and text composition by Ellen Rosenblatt/SD Designs

CONTENTS

EVERYONE IS WORKING HARDER THAN EVER AND TIME HAS NEVER seemed to slip by so fast. Why should a busy business professional take time to read *The New Successful Large Account Management*? What is in it for you? The answer is that, short of an MBA course, this is the quickest and most comprehensive way to unravel the mysteries of successful large account development, showing you how to target, understand, and partner with key clients, profitably and for the long term.

Over the past ten years everyone in business has become knowledgeable about managing costs and improving the bottom line. Far fewer people have focused on the equally critical area of how to grow the top line, not just with one advertising campaign or big push but for real growth, year in and year out. When the CEO's path to the top of large global corporations is examined, only in a few cases did they spend critical time in sales and business development.

In the next ten years much more emphasis will be placed on business development skills. There will be any number of miracle sales methods launched, which will have the life span of the average new diet plan. At Aon, we are already ahead of the curve because Miller Heiman has distilled common sense, practical experience, and some innovative thinking to allow us the benefit of the LAMP advantage.

In line with most global companies, we are driven by a "client first" focus. The challenge is to translate this from good intentions to practical actions that demonstrate and deliver value to the client consistently. It has become rare for a single producer or relationship manager to be able to develop large accounts on his or her own. In the complex world of the twenty-first century people's talents are more specialized, so that we have entered the realm of team selling. How to communicate goals and strategy to this team becomes critical, but even more important is how to tap into the creative energy that everyone brings to a project. The Large Account Management Process allows this energy to be harnessed and focused on the whole client relationship. Miller Heiman understands that, even as client industry specialization has become accepted best practice, it is often still seen as a smoke screen for selling more of our "stuff." They know that, without a deep commitment to what makes our clients successful in their business, there can be no long-term partnership.

Quick hits often turn out to be very costly mistakes. To target and win significant business from a Large Account today you must be prepared to invest heavily in research, in building a relationship, in assembling a team, and in responding thoughtfully to an opportunity. We need to apply the same rigorous analysis to the investment we are making in that client as we would if we were allocating capital to purchase new equipment or open a new office. In the past this has often been done on the basis of one person's relationship or something that worked for us before. Now managers and individual teams have a much more reliable method of prioritizing and quantifying key accounts. LAMP has been a great reference point for our best developers but, equally importantly, a trusty guide for all levels of our sales staff. The standard complaint in business is that there are not enough skilled sales leaders available, so the challenge is to realize the potential of everyone engaged in this exciting adventure. LAMP delivers!

For Aon the Large Account Management Process has enabled us to grow talent by bringing all elements of development into clear focus and allowing us to drive the relationship to give the result that benefits both us and the client, consistently and for the long term.

Patrick Thomas,
Development Director for Global and Strategic Accounts,
AON RISK SERVICES INTERNATIONAL

ACKNOWLEDGMENTS

OUR THANKS FIRST AND FOREMOST TO MILLER HEIMAN COO DAMON Jones, who made significant contributions of his time and expertise, helped to review and refine *The New Successful Large Account Management*'s many revisions, and served as an invaluable resource during the entire production process. We are grateful also to Nick Speare and Jon Zimmermann for their careful editing and for major contributions of concept and methodology; and to our literary agent, Lila Karpf.

In addition, we owe a debt of gratitude to our clients, our business partners, and our sales consultants for the LAMP experiences that they graciously contributed.

Customers who shared stories with us included Bill Clement, Director of Enterprise Development for Siemens Building Technologies; Ged Holmes, former Director of Business Sales for O2; Tony Leach, Sales Director at Experian; Don McKelvie, Director of Worldwide Sales for Baker Atlas; Neville Seabridge, Sales Director at Experian; Ben Vreeburg, Sales Director at Loders Croklaan; and Paul Wichman, Vice President of Sales for Schwab Institutional. Patrick Thomas, Development Director for Global and Strategic Accounts at Aon Risk Services International, not only shared his considerable experience and expertise, but also was kind enough to write the Foreword. Our sincere appreciation, too, to Lisa Napolitano, President and CEO of the Strategic Account Management Association, for her thoughtful and illuminating Epilogue.

For their LAMP insights, we also thank Miller Heiman sales consultants Jerry Barnes, Tony Ellis, Ian Irving, Mike Joyce, Michael Light, Vince McFarlane, Mickey O'Callaghan, Mark Sellers, Raiyo Shroff, Pam Switzer, and Jim Watkins. A special note of gratitude to Sharon Williams for her project-development support, contributions of concept and methodology, and for her fifteen-year commitment to Miller Heiman excellence.

Back to Growth

"It's not just about your business. It's based on a committed strategy to support the customer's success."

—Sam Reese,

President and Chief Executive Officer, Miller Heiman

COMPETITIVE PRESSURE ON COMPANIES HAS NEVER BEEN GREATER. GLOBalization, mergers and acquisitions, eroding margins, outsourcing, the technological revolution, shrinking customer bases—these and other developments are creating unprecedented challenges for business managers, especially for those who manage strategic accounts. More than ever, maintaining and building relationships with these key customers has become essential to sustaining the P&L profile that you need to survive and grow.

There are two approaches to maintaining a healthy P&L. Cut costs or improve revenue. (Ideally, of course, you do both.) By now the first approach, which dominated corporate strategies throughout the 1990s, is approaching the stage of limited returns, as organizations realize that there's only so much excess any company can cut out. As a result the second approach, revenue improvement, is fast becoming a universal imperative. Recognizing that revenue is the lifeblood of their organizations, managers increasingly are following the mantra "back to growth."

There are two approaches for a business intent on growing

revenue. Expand into new markets and new customer bases, or optimize the business you have in your existing accounts. These approaches are meant to be complementary, but with global competition severely curtailing market expansion, leading firms are focusing on the second option, seeking to develop untapped potential in their existing customer bases. Alert to the traditional benchmark that 50 percent of a company's revenue comes from 5 percent of its customers, they are concentrating on that critical 5 percent—the accounts that companies define variously as their key, strategic, or simply "large" accounts. Even small businesses are following this pattern, by focusing on those critical accounts that are large *to them*.

There are two approaches to improving business with your Large Accounts. The old-fashioned method is to try to sell them more and bill them accordingly. A more reliable method, as measured by enhanced revenue over the long term, is to work on building relationships that bring the accounts *value*. In fact the single "secret" to business success in the twenty-first century is to make contributions to your key accounts that ensure *their* success.

The New Successful Large Account Management shows how to get this done. Distilling decades of Miller Heiman experience in strategic account management, it discusses in detail exactly what we deliver in our globally renowned private and public LAMP sessions. It explains, for example:

- Why you must manage your Large Accounts like "external assets."
- How to identify a manageable Field of Play within the account.
- Why differentiation is a function of customer perception.
- How to resist the incessant push toward commoditization.
- How to draft a Charter Statement that gets customer endorsement.
- How to coordinate qualitative Goals with quantitative revenue.

- How to optimize the internal allocation of limited resources.
- How to deliver customer value that ensures long-term success.

The need for a reliable account management process is more urgent today than it has ever been. If you doubt that, try to find an institutional banker with less than a 30 percent churn rate or a telecom that doesn't worry about customer switching. And this in a world where, marketing experts estimate, it costs *six times as much* to reacquire an unhappy customer as it does to keep a satisfied one on board. Clearly, maintaining what market analyst Frederick Reichheld calls the Loyalty Effect has become a make-or-break proposition for businesses today.*

At Miller Heiman, we have been promoting the Loyalty Effect for two decades with the Large Account Management Process (LAMP) described in this book. When we first introduced this process, few customers had a robust strategic account management system in place. Today, according to the Strategic Account Management Association, about two out of three companies have SAM programs in place, yet many of these organizations are still struggling to realize real returns from these programs, because they lack a coherent *process* for managing Large Accounts. It is the pragmatic reliance on such a process that differentiates LAMP.

We have delivered the lessons of LAMP to thousands of account executives around the world, and their feedback has left no doubt that our process-oriented approach pays off. In better penetration of existing customers; better retention; better use of internal resources; and better, more predictable positioning as a valued strategic partner on what we call the Buy-Sell Hierarchy. That's why major organizations are still sending their

---

*The Loyalty Effect (Cambridge: Harvard University Press, 1996).

best people to us. Why we can count among our valued LAMP veterans such global leaders as AT&T, Experian, Pepsi, Siemens, and Schwab.

Although the basic principles of the process we teach these clients have remained constant, in a world of moving targets you must adapt or perish. Therefore, as the business landscape has continued to display volatility, we have responded. We have listened carefully to our customers, just as we advise them to listen to their customers, and have profited continually from their experiences and their feedback. We've listened to our own sales consultants, too, learning which LAMP concepts bring the "Aha's!" and which ones need clarification. And we've fed the insights of both customers and sales consultants back into the process. As a result, LAMP today is more granular, nuanced, and practical than it ever has been.

One of the key insights we have gained from customers and colleagues is that, to maintain a high return on your relationship investment, you must make it crystal clear to your major customers that you are managing their accounts for *mutual* advantage—for the robust growth of *their* businesses, not just your own. We consider this insight so important that we have made it the basic premise of this book:

Basic Premise of LAMP

To achieve long-term profitable relationships with your key customers, you must make consistent, measurable contributions to *their* profitability and *their* customer relationships.

What LAMP delivers, and what you'll find described in this book, is a systematic method for defining and leveraging the resources you need to ensure that both your and your customers' businesses thrive.

The New Successful Large Account Management builds on many other, equally useful insights from our corporate clients. Here you'll discover, in their own words, how many of these "process experts" apply LAMP to their own account management challenges, in strategic arenas as different as institutional finance, telecommunications, and retail. You'll see, too, how the flexibility of the LAMP process makes it relevant not just to large firms like our Fortune 500 clients, but to small- and mid-sized businesses, too—many of which have been able to leverage its principles to gain the LAMP advantage against powerful competitors.

Whatever their size and whatever their markets, businesses everywhere need to protect their key account "assets." They need to deliver real customer value or risk being "de-positioned" as commodity suppliers. They need to invest appropriately in the strategic relationships that are the only safeguard against account erosion. LAMP has helped literally thousands of account team members address these fundamental needs, with field-tested, measurable results across multiple industries.

In this book, which reflects the input of thousands of experienced users, we present this unique account management process as we teach it today. With profound thanks to these customers and colleagues, we offer it as a *Common Sense* for twenty-first-century business—a prototype for thinking about accounts, relationships, and competitive advantage in an era when "back to growth" has become a watchword for survival.

PART I

Basic Principles

CHAPTER 1

The New Landscape of Account Management: Eight Lessons

"Change alone is unchanging."

—Heraclitus

IN THE PAST FEW DECADES, ACCOUNT MANAGEMENT HAS BEEN TRANS-formed by the most incredible explosion of technological wizardry to appear since the Scientific Revolution of the seventeenth century. Today, even small- to medium-sized firms routinely equip their sales, marketing, and account management people with Web sites, intranets, mobile phones, call centers, PDAs, and e-mail. These aren't options. They're widely acknowledged to constitute an essential, bare-minimum tool set for the twenty-first century. If you don't have these tools today, you're probably not in business.

Yet, contrary to what its providers would like us to believe, the new technology does not in itself provide competitive advantage. In fact, the very ubiquity of information and communications technology (ICT) systems means that owning the tools themselves is merely an entry fee—something that your company needs to even be in the game. If you're competing for major account revenue today, therefore, you've got to rely on something other than the latest generation of IT products and services.

There are multiple, interconnected aspects to that "something other," but one thread ties them all together. To achieve competitive advantage today, especially in targeting large or "strategic" accounts, the key differentiating factor is the ability to build relationships that bring your customers measurable value over time. In a sense there's nothing new about this imperative; bringing customers value has always been a key to success. But the world in which we now must do this has in fact changed—and changed in ways that are only marginally related to technology.

These changes present significant challenges to business professionals, and in this opening chapter we'll detail the most important ones. These are the "field position changes" that, as an account manager or member of an account team, you need to be thinking about before you can even begin to draft plans for approaching your Large Accounts. We present them here as eight essential lessons.

Lesson One: Technology Changes Everything

While good account management, like good selling, has always depended on effective information management, in today's hyper-connected, information-saturated, wireless environment, that requirement has been pushed to an entirely new level. Not only is there now infinitely *more* information out there than ever before, but that information is both instantly and ubiquitously *accessible*. Now, thanks to Google, Yahoo!, Hoover's, and a host of other unlikely-named databanks and search engines, the newest market entrants can acquire, within minutes, the kind of rich customer data that used to take days, and that pre-Web sales and marketing teams could only dream about. Which means that, with very little investment of either time or money, they can acquire as much public information about your accounts as you have yourselves.

Private information, of course, is another matter—and showing you how to get that information is a large part of this book. But as far as the public domain goes, with few exceptions, it has never been easier to become knowledgeable about what makes businesses tick—what's worrying their executives, what markets they're investigating, where they're being hammered by competitors, what new products they're bringing to market. All of this stuff is available at click speed—to you, to your current competitors, and to all those new potential players.

Here's another hard truth: Your customers have access to this new information, too. They're using it to research your capabilities, to compare them against those of your competitors, and to bring to the bargaining table a much higher degree of sophistication than businesses have ever had to contend with before. The accounts that you acquired fairly easily during the 1990s boom are both more resource-poor and data-rich than they were then—and fully capable of using that scenario to *their* competitive advantage.

The information bonanza that Web developers are fond of bragging about, therefore, has brought account managers an opportunity that is also a challenge. It's a much more open field than it was a decade ago, but one in which the pure volume of information that technology makes available can become a problem in itself. So, to help you sort the wheat from the chaff, rather than gathering more data just for the sake of gathering it, you need an information management system that can help you transform all that free-floating data into usable business knowledge.

Lesson Two: Technology Changes Nothing

By information management system, we don't mean software. Perhaps the greatest single mistake of the dot-com years was the idea that technology in itself was going to make us all rich. In pursuit of that dream, company after company invested heavily in software that was designed to "automate" the sales and marketing process. First it was Sales Force Automation (SFA), then Customer Relationship Management (CRM), and then Enterprise Relationship Management (ERM). Some companies did very well with these new systems, but a shockingly large percentage of these fixes fell flat, bringing little to no returns on massive IT investments.

Systems failed for three related reasons. First, the purchasing companies allowed themselves to believe that the software would somehow run itself, and therefore failed to invest adequately in the ancillary services that CRM providers were only too eager to sell them—services like integration assistance, data cleansing, and most importantly training. Second, poorly trained and often suspicious sales and marketing people decided that the new "automation" software was just another gimmick—and one that would require them to enter data while getting nothing in return. So they just didn't use it—a phenomenon that became known in Silicon Valley as the "user adoption problem." Third, many companies, intoxicated by CRM's shiny bells and supersonic whistles, failed to analyze the processes that they were automating; what they got, therefore, was the same old selling blunders, only faster.

The lesson isn't to avoid CRM software, or any other technology. Used properly, good software can be as effective an account management tool as a clear-signal mobile phone or a broadband connection. But that's all it is. Software can no more turn an incompetent salesperson into a double-quota winner than a $200 driver can turn your average five-year-old into Tiger Woods. Results are never provided by a tool in itself. They're provided by the effective use of that tool in the hands of a professional who follows a replicable, tested *process* for ensuring success, and who knows that, however sophisticated your toolbox, it's still the effective management of *relationships* that drives long-term business.

That's an old lesson, of course. We've been teaching it in all our programs for more than twenty years. It bears repeating here because today, perhaps more than ever before, you *need* good tools to keep your competitive edge, and it's easy to be fooled into believing that they'll do the job for you. Because we know they won't, we focus in this book, as in our programs, on defining an account management process that is generalizable—a process for building solid, mutually beneficial relationships that can be supported by whatever technology you adopt.

Lesson Three: Customers Are Still in Charge

In the early days of the Internet, the more optimistic champions of online commerce predicted that, sooner or later, all transactions would move to this lower-cost channel, and the centuries-old brick-and-mortar model would become obsolete. The fact that this didn't happen tells us something critical about customer psychology—something that has tremendous implications for Large Account management.

What Internet transactions offer people isn't so much a replacement for their customary buying and selling behavior as an expansion of choices—this explains their popularity. Sometimes customers go online to make actual purchases on the spot; pioneering Web business leaders like Amazon built their reputations by offering that service. But even in some other leading online firms, like the electronic brokerage Charles Schwab, a heavy proportion of trading happens offline—at the branch offices that some individuals prefer. Some customers, moreover, use the Web as a research tool, gathering comparative data about prospective purchases and potential suppliers that enables them to make more informed buying decisions. And not all the decisions they make favor buying online.

In fact, over the past few years, airline and hotel customers, to pick only the most obvious examples, have become adept at using the Web as a bargaining tool. Armed with a low online quote, they can more effectively demand deeper discounts in the brick-and-mortar world. A similar comparison-shopping strategy works on the B2B level, where Internet auctions have dramatically intensified competition for corporate contracts.

Whether you're looking at individual consumers or Large Accounts, the outcome is the same. Even though only a relatively small portion of today's business takes place online, the mere presence of the Web as an alternate transaction channel has upped the ante for suppliers across all channels. The hard fact for businesses, online or off, is that *the Internet makes customers more discerning and more demanding.* Because they have become used to the instant, personalized, and cheaper responses available on the Web, they have come to expect equivalent levels of speed and service wherever they do business. One of the great ironies of the computer age is that machines have made customers more insistent on personal responsiveness.

For all businesses, therefore, the old adage about the customer always being right has taken on a special urgency. Customers today have been "reconditioned" by the Web. They are better informed, more aware of their options, and therefore more empowered than customers have ever been before. Making matters even more challenging in the B2B world is the fact that, when customers are asked to identify vendors' shortcomings, the single biggest complaint they make, according to HR Chally research, is that salespeople don't understand their businesses. This can have a chilling effect on customer receptivity. And, in more situations than most of us would like to admit, it means that the old loyalty effect is a fleeting phenomenon.

In fact, customer defection, or "churn," is a major problem everywhere. In the telecommunications industry, which coined the term, it's particularly severe. Our client Ged Holmes, who implemented LAMP when he was head of business sales at the British mobile network leader O2, cites "staggering" industry churn averages of between 18 and 24 percent. "It's only through a tremendously disciplined approach to the account as a whole," he says, "that telcom providers are able to keep that under control. You've got to realize that your job isn't to write new contracts, but to sustain the profitability of the business you already have. In a customer-centric world, that's a constant challenge. And the only way you can meet it is to respond to customers' demands for consultative service. It's not about giving them more technology. It's about using technology to help them plan the future."

Lesson Four: Short Lists Are Getting Shorter

The rise of supply chain management, both as a technology and as a business strategy, has fundamentally altered the way suppliers are obliged to do business. A dozen years ago, your proposal might be judged based largely on its intrinsic merits: price, product reputation, compliance with an RFP's specs, ability to deliver against a deadline, and so on. That's no longer enough. Today's leading corporations are systematically gauging the *total cost of doing business* with their competing suppliers—and are moving toward ever shorter short lists of those who make the grade. This conscious *narrowing of the vendor base* is happening across the board, whether the cost to be covered entails a communications network, office supplies, or a potentially outsourceable HR function.

For anyone trying to manage a Large Account, the widespread adoption of supply chain management means that procurement has become a central factor in sales. As procurement specialists look for ever more ingenious ways to trim costs, the natural tendency—often a conscious one—is toward commoditization. This tendency, increasingly, is becoming quite scientific. Not only do companies rely on back-office automation systems to drive personnel costs out of routine procurements. In addition, many European firms now tap the resources of purchasing institutes to help them rationalize the supply chain management process. And the largest firms maintain huge procurement departments, specifically tasked by the C level to drive costs down.

Don McKelvie, a LAMP client and Director of Worldwide Sales of the leading oilfield service supplier Baker Atlas, notes that the procurement specialty has emerged, at least in part, as a result of the merger and acquisitions mania. "In the acquisitions process," he points out, "many oil companies spent millions of dollars more than the acquired company's assets were worth. One way of showing Wall Street that the resulting synergy justifies their investment is to hammer their suppliers into volume discounts. This is why the super majors and some larger independent oil companies pay literally hundreds of employees to manage procurement. That creates a challenge for vendors, because some procurement departments justify their entire existence by pushing suppliers down into a commodity position."

In the new procurement-driven world, "getting out of commodity" is a major challenge. We'll address it throughout this book, and especially in Chapter 4, when we speak about maintaining your position on the Buy-Sell Hierarchy.

Lesson Five: It's Not About Making the Sale

In an arena where every buyer impulse is driving you toward commodity, focusing on individual transactions only ensures that status. To ensure success—even survival—in today's Large Account arena, you've got to set your sights on three or four years out, and on building long-term business, not just today's "opportunities." The reason is logical enough: Adding up quick serial wins gets you perceived as shortsighted, while working for the account's long-term benefit helps to ensure account retention. And in today's environment, retention is the name of the game.

Bill Clement is Director of Enterprise Development for Siemens Building Technologies. He draws a good distinction between companies that are truly relation-based, or customer-centric, and those that he calls "opportunistic." "In an opportunistic company," he says, "you work from quarter to quarter at best, and sometimes even from deal to deal or, in our industry, what I'd call from project to project. In other words, you focus on single opportunities, and this tends to make you in the worst sense opportunistic. When you approach business this way, it's difficult to leverage your successes, because you don't see the relationships you're building as part of a larger, account management picture." Without such a picture, as Clement rightly insists, the best project management in the world will bring only limited returns.

The reason is that, in Large Account management today,

successful firms help their clients *run their businesses*—not just purchase supplies or utilize services. The overall goal of any good LAMP process is to ensure better business returns for the targeted Large Account. This means keeping the focus not on your customer per se, but on *your customer's customers*—the accounts or consumers and other stakeholders that, over time, are making your Large Account successful. It means asking, regularly, how a given initiative or sale ties in to the Large Account's overall business strategy.

Experian Sales Director Neville Seabridge articulates this well when he talks about information. "Businesses have loads of information about their clients, including marketing information. But they seldom have enough information about those clients' own marketing problems, and that's an important area to concentrate on. Rather than selling products into customer organizations, the real challenge is to understand their pain points, their problems with customer retention, and deliver solutions that will alleviate those problems."

The central lesson of any truly Win-Win business is that your success is a function of your customers' success. Not for this quarter alone, but for the long haul. Businesses are successful over time because they add value to their customers' businesses while simultaneously realizing value themselves. Only this kind of mutual benefit justifies continued investment in a relationship. To many senior-level people, who must answer to shareholders quarter to quarter, this is a difficult lesson to act on, especially when markets are volatile: Some of them frankly still see long-term account management as an investment that they're making in their successors' careers. But it's a valid lesson nonetheless. And the narrowing of the vendor base makes it an all the more urgent imperative.

Lesson Six: Account Management Is Business Management

A generation ago, an "account manager" was understood, often disparagingly, as someone who managed the relatively nondemanding work of follow-up and service—non-revenue-producing tasks like handling complaint calls, taking clients to lunch, and providing documentation. Today, in top firms you get to manage a major account only *after* you've proved your effectiveness in the selling arena. You've got dedicated responsibilities for overseeing all aspects of the relationship with the account—including both P&L and relational aspects. You may have an office at the customer's site, and "live" there part of the time. You're the account's advocate in your own organization—so much so that, in some companies, top management may sometimes wonder about whether or not you've "gone native." You're aware, in fact, that you have to manage your company's perception of your loyalty—and never promise the Large Account anything that you aren't sure your firm will be willing to deliver.

As a Large Account manager today, in fact, you function less like a salesperson than like a business development specialist or general manager—roles that require much different skill sets than most salespeople possess. You run a team of professionals whose responsibilities, like yours, are focused virtually exclusively on one account. That account is, in a real sense, your external asset—a kind of extended business unit of the parent organization. You've therefore moved beyond selling. Your compensation and influence reflect your senior role. So do the expectations that your company has of you. You've got a quota that reflects the importance of the "business" you manage. You may have P&L responsibilities. And you've got the resources, on your own say-so, to get the job done.

This scenario, which is already a reality in many Fortune 500 and other leading firms, is destined to become more and more typical. The wave of the future is clear: Large Account management is becoming a senior management function, driven by executive vision and appropriate resource allocation devoted to building relationships that in some cases develop into actual joint venture partnerships and that in all cases must deliver real customer value. Only this approach provides safeguards against customer defection. If your company isn't moving in that direction, you're already behind the curve.

Lesson Seven: The Lone Ranger Has Left the Building

When we started teaching LAMP in the late 1980s only the largest of our clients—firms like Hewlett-Packard and AT&T—utilized the integrated skills of designated teams to manage their ongoing relationships with Large Accounts. Today that has become a best practice across multiple industries. The days are past when a single person could hold all the relevant information about an account in his head and manage it as his private turf. Today, account management requires the coordinated effort of cross-functional teams, composed not just of salespeople, but also of people from a wide range of support and service areas. There are four points that are important to remember about these teams.

First, other than a small core, the team is typically made up of ad hoc rather than permanent members. Since it is designed to meet the account's needs in a dynamic environment, its composition—and the responsibilities of its members—have to be flexible. Once an account team gets locked into a permanent, graven-in-stone position on a corporate org chart, it loses its ability to respond to the needs of the client. One of the main challenges facing account managers today is how to coordinate the activities of these flexible entities.

Second, the best account teams are carefully and consciously aligned with the customer's teams. Team best practice today means working regularly with the Large Account to understand its changing needs—and placing your people face-to-face with the appropriate people in the account, to quickly and most effectively respond to those needs.

Third, because people only do effectively what they're rewarded for doing, the compensation structure of a Large Account team must respond to the differential input of *all* the team members, not just the superstar Lone Rangers who ride in at the end of the quarter and close the big deals. Large Account management is not a "sales function." If you want it to work, you must reward everybody who contributes.

Fourth, the team must have the internal resources and authority to function for the client as a resource provider. To do so effectively, it must have the executive support and interdepartmental clout to meet the client's needs instantly when they arise. This is why, in many companies, top managers serve as executive sponsors and active team members, often meeting with their executive counterparts on the customer side. Without the leverage provided by executive involvement, teams can easily fall victim to the deadly trap of overpromising and underdelivering. And herein lies one of the great advantages of the LAMP process. In the words of one client, "LAMP is the best tool for marshaling internal resources that our firm has ever seen."

Lesson Eight: You Ain't Seen Nothing Yet

The final lesson, while it speaks especially to the momentous changes of the past decade and a half, also goes back to a principle that we identified in our very first corporate program, Strategic Selling. It's that whatever got you where you are today will not be enough to keep you there as we go forward. Change will continue to be the only constant, and the pace of change will continue to accelerate. Therefore, the absolute essential for a good account management program is to have a process planning tool that is flexible enough to respond not only to the challenges that you're already facing, but also to those you haven't yet imagined.

Information technology specialists are fond of quoting Moore's Law—a rule of thumb defined by Intel co-founder Gordon Moore that computer capability, in terms of chip speed, increases by a factor of two every eighteen months. However accurate this estimate may be, it points to an immensely important fact that far transcends the specifics of computing capacity. It's that, in an ICT-dominated world, change proceeds exponentially, not arithmetically. Which means that, however rapidly the business environment has been changing up to now, we ain't seen nothing yet.

We're in no better position than anyone else to tell you what the next ten years will bring. But we can say one thing for certain. In an exponentially morphing world, you need flexible tools—tools that will help you meet tomorrow's challenges, whatever they may prove to be. The planning process that we describe in this book is one of those indispensable tools.

CHAPTER 2

Selecting the Large Account

"There are serious opportunities for bottom-line improvement by serving the right strategic accounts."

—Sallie Sherman, Joseph Sperry, and Samuel Reese*

WHAT ARE THE "RIGHT" STRATEGIC ACCOUNTS? OF THE SEVERAL LARGE Accounts that provide your company with critical revenue, how do you decide which ones are the best candidates for partnering relationships and therefore for LAMP analysis? Traditionally, Miller Heiman has answered that question by giving both a qualitative and a quantitative definition.

Qualitatively, we've said, "large" means large in *importance*—importance to you and to your business, however you measure that. Quantitatively, we've pointed to a widely observed statistical pattern: the fact that, over time and across multiple industries, 5 percent of any company's customers typically bring in at least 50 percent of their business. And we've said that the quantitative definition reinforces the qualitative one. If an account, of whatever size, falls into a 5 percent "core" that is crucial to your company, it clearly provides an opportunity that you cannot afford to neglect.

---

*The Seven Keys to Managing Strategic Accounts (New York: McGraw-Hill, 2003), p. 76.

Today, although importance and the "5 percent pattern" remain valid criteria, it's useful to have greater specificity with regard to account selection. In a world where profit margins are already razor-thin and where customers are putting increasing pressure on vendors to deliver value-added solutions, you need something more than a statistical benchmark and your own gut feelings—however reliable—to help you identify the accounts that matter most to your company. You need reliable selection criteria for the twenty-first century. Unfortunately, despite the plethora of segmentation guides now straining the bookshelves, many companies that recognize the importance of their Large Accounts still have only very foggy notions—in some cases counterproductive notions—about how to identify the best ones for strategic analysis.

How Not to Select a Large Account

In part, the confusion results from organizational complexity. In a company where 20 people may interact with every large customer, and where there are two hundred customers, it's pretty difficult to get consensus about what criteria matter consistently, across the organization and its various market segments. As a result, it's common for companies trying to develop their strategic accounts to draft selection criteria that resemble a ten-year-old's Christmas list.

The endless wish list. In a survey that we conducted with S4 Consulting, for example, one client named 150 distinct criteria that were in use for strategic account selection. These ranged from the obvious, like revenue potential and competitive advantage, to the relatively arcane, like a "common raw materials base" and "potential process synergy."* But even if every one of the 150 criteria made sense to someone in the company, there were just too many of them to be useful, company-wide. So one of the first things to ensure when you're

---

*The Seven Keys to Managing Strategic Accounts, p. 77.

thinking about selecting an account for Large Account treatment is that all the members of your team who will be involved with this account buy in, with enthusiasm, to the criteria you're using. In other words, that you all agree on *why* this account is important. In achieving that, the fewer criteria, the better.

Everybody can't be "strategic." In the old days of "selling by the numbers," the guiding philosophy was that all revenue was alike, and that there was no such thing as a poor sale or an unwanted customer. That sounds laughably antiquated today, yet tradition dies hard, and many organizations that have abandoned the old mantra "Any sale is a good sale" still harbor the notion that all customers—all big customers, anyway—should be managed as if they were "strategic." In a world of limited resources, this can't happen. Trying to make it happen will undermine not only the "Treat everybody like a king" approach, but also the proper management of those customers who *could* be strategic. Not least of all, it will irritate the mid-level customers who you said you would treat like key accounts, and then found that you couldn't.

"Trying to focus on too many customers," say the authors of *The Seven Keys to Managing Strategic Accounts*, "is an excellent way to waste valuable resources."* Ged Holmes, former head of business sales at O2 and a LAMP expert, agrees. "When you're managing a territory with a lot of accounts," he says, "you've got to adopt a cut-down approach, so your people aren't doing Large Account planning for more than they can handle. We've found that a ratio of one rep to five accounts, or maybe one to ten, is appropriate—you can still focus on the few accounts that will prove profitable. Beyond that it starts to get unwieldy."

There's a connection, of course, between using too many account selection criteria and selecting too many accounts for special treatment. The more criteria you're using, the more

---

*The Seven Keys to Managing Strategic Accounts, p. 66.

likely it is that an account which is of marginal value based on one criterion will look like a potential partner based on another one. That's why you need to refine your selection criteria down to a "best few."

Revenue isn't everything. Common sense might dictate that, whatever other criteria you use, the first of the best few criteria should be revenue. Common sense would be wrong. Certainly, revenue is important, but only as part of a broader picture—one that logically and practically has to include things like enhanced brand recognition, greater market penetration, and sustainable profitability. Consider the key account customer who demands an unreasonable share of your limited resources, who is unduly costly to service, or who—on a "softer" level—is psychologically stressful for your people to work with. Does it make sense to focus extraordinary effort on that kind of high-revenue customer? Maybe. But before concluding that such a customer "obviously" deserves special treatment, you would be wise to calculate the indirect costs of that business. Sometimes a revenue plus can be an ROI negative.

Neither are blue-ribbon accounts. Not every household-name account is necessarily a good candidate for Large Account treatment. Patrick Thomas, the Development Director for Global and Strategic Accounts at the insurance and risk management leader Aon, puts it this way: "Sometimes, the more analysis you do the more potential trouble you find. While Fortune 500 accounts do have a lot of money to pay out in consultant fees and advisors, they also demand their pound of flesh and they know exactly what they are getting for their money. If you don't manage the relationship very carefully, you could find yourselves facing very large losses."

It's worth keeping this in mind when the marquee lights dazzle you. We've all seen instances in which a name brand owner holds its smaller suppliers hostage, expecting that its global reputation justifies special treatment. The reality is that, for every small vendor who enjoys a market boost because Big Cola or Big Auto is on its customer list, another one has to explain to his stockholders why owning that prestige account has become a P&L liability. With big names as with big money, the lesson is the same: An account only deserves the royal treatment if it treats *you* like royalty.

A two-way street. Which brings us to the most important lesson of all. At Miller Heiman, we've built a reputation championing the Win-Win concept, and it's a concept that is directly relevant to Large Account management—and therefore to Large Account selection. Relationship alignment is a critical feature of Large Account selection, for only those relationships whose value is recognized by both supplier and customer are truly sustainable. If either party fails to understand that value, the relationship will become unbalanced, and efforts to stay Win-Win will inevitably falter.

In identifying which accounts deserve a Large Account approach, therefore, you have to start by assessing current or potential mutuality. This means that, in addition to gauging what benefits a strategic relationship could bring your company, you must spend equal time gauging the benefits that such a relationship could bring to your customer. And you must do this from the *account's point of view*. This is easier to say than to do, because in going after Large Accounts, most of us are all too quick to grab the rose-colored glasses, and to assume that what we see as added value will be obvious to the customer. Often, it's not.

Determining whether a strategic relationship with Zeno Industries would bring your company value is hard enough. Determining whether it would profit Zeno is much harder, because only Zeno people can give you the answer. We'll be talking throughout this book about the need for continual assessment of your accounts' perceptions—and we'll be giving you guidelines for performing such assessment. Suffice it to say here that, until you know with some precision what the Zeno people perceive to be the value of the relationship, you are on thin ice calling them a Large Account.

So much for the common mistakes that organizations make in selecting Large Accounts. How do you do it right? At Miller

Heiman, we answer that question by encouraging our clients to perform three sequential forms of account analysis:

• First, as a *preliminary diagnosis*, we ask them to identify not their clear "winner" accounts, but those where something seems a little bit "off"—that is, where the revenue or the relationship, or both, are underperforming. We recommend this as a safeguard against the all-too-common "strategy" of devoting the lion's share of your attention to the easy sells—very seldom an approach that consistently builds business.

• Second, we ask them to subject their customer lists to a *portfolio analysis*—assessing their customers against performance and performance-potential criteria to zero in on those that are most likely to deliver the long-term profitable relationships that LAMP supports.

• Finally, we ask them to zero in on a manageable portion of the Large Account—a segment that we call a Field of Play.

Preliminary Diagnosis

A good Large Account analysis brings clarity into chaos by helping businesses better organize their information. For this reason, such a process is particularly valuable when your information is unclear—where, in spite of good revenue, you feel confused about where a major account may be going. Because gut feelings of uncertainty should always be taken seriously, we recommend that, as you work through this book, you target first one of your less-than-perfect accounts. Not only will you get more out of working in a "gray" account, but this is the type of account where you *need* it most. It's painfully easy to find yourself behind the eight ball when you ignore your sense that "something" is wrong. So, in identifying those Large Accounts that are "due" for LAMP analysis, you should begin by bringing to the surface hidden problems *before* they have a chance to become overwhelming. To help you perform this kind of preventive diagnosis, we suggest you ask yourself these questions:

1. Has there been any inconsistency in your planning for this account, over geography or over time? Do you and your company have a consistent plan for handling this Large Account's various regional (or international) business units? Do you understand how the units fit together? Or do the organizational and purchasing structures of the parent account sometimes seem like impenetrable labyrinths? What about time? Does your account planning show a purposeful *evolution* from one year and one quarter to the next? If this quarter's plan looks exactly like last quarter's, that's pretty good evidence that there's something ineffective about your strategy. The same thing is true if each quarter's plan shows virtually no connection with what came before.

2. Do your account strategies ever fail to impact, positively and indisputably, on your company's revenues and profitability? What's the perceived link between your strategies and the income the account delivers? Can you document that link, or are you guessing? Do you have a clear understanding of how the account got to be "large"? Or did it "just get that way" by momentum? Perhaps most important of all, do the strategies that you adopt for this account impact positively on *its* revenue? If the relationship you've established so far isn't showing up on the *customer's* bottom line, he or she may be a top candidate for LAMP analysis.

3. How reliable is your company's system for reviewing and measuring account plans? If an account plan is working (or not working), how early does your company know it? How frequently, and in how disciplined a fashion, do you track progress on individual objectives for this Large Account? If a given goal proves unrealistic, can you regroup and reset quickly? Do you have a process for involving your valued customers in the testing of your goals? Or are you sometimes left hanging, planning mid-course corrections on your own and too late to help you?

4. Do you ever lack the budget to do the job? Is there a reasonable degree of congruity between your account plans and the resources that they require? Does your company's top management understand that this Large Account is critical not just to your success, but to the success of the firm? Are you usually able to convince them that the expected return on investment from this account justifies spending resources up front? And are those resources, once committed, being allocated effectively? If an account shows "penny wise but pound foolish" resource allocation, it may be a good candidate for Large Account treatment.

5. *Are you insecure in your position?* Do you feel confident that you understand this Large Account and your place in it as "external manager"? Do you know who makes decisions, and on what grounds? Have you fully explored sales possibilities in the account beyond those currently on the table? What about the competition? How firm is your position compared to theirs? And—most important of all—*do you know how decision makers in the Large Account feel about your place in their business?* If you're not sure what they feel—or if you're unsure about any other aspect of your position—mark this up as a major gray area.

We urge you to be brutally honest in your responses to these diagnostic questions and to trust your instincts as well as your head. Isolate those Large Accounts where you are uncertain about your position. Then move on to the second phase of analysis.

Portfolio Analysis

Good financial management means constant asset assessment, and the frequent selection and de-selection of portfolio items, to capture the greatest possible advantage in volatile markets. The same principle applies in the management of your "external assets." Large Accounts can be no less volatile than stock prices, so you have to approach their management with equal due diligence, and subject them to frequent analysis of their value to your company. Never is this analysis more important than when you're trying to determine which items in your customer "portfolio" should receive the special commitment of Large Account planning. Making an account "strategic" is going to cost you funds and other resources. Naturally, you want this outlay to bring you a reliable return. To maximize the chances of that occurring, we recommend that the people involved with each LAMP "candidate" convene to develop answers to the following questions and issues:

1. Revenue. What revenue has this account brought in over the past year? The past two or three years? What revenue do you realistically project that it will bring in over the next two or three years? You should look here not only at the total revenue flow, but also how the revenue picture breaks down in terms of different locations, corporate divisions, business units, or product lines. This nuance will help you define whether a particular segment of the corporate entity is the most promising strategic arena. We'll clarify this point later in the chapter, when we explain Field of Play.

2. Costs. What are the annual average costs of doing business with this account? Not just the costs of the goods or services you supply, but also the costs of sales, support, and account management. Again, focus not just on total costs but on as granular a breakdown as you can achieve in terms of organizational structure and geography. Subtract costs from revenues to estimate your margins, and you may be surprised to find that some of your high-rolling customers are actually draining your profits. When one of S4 Consulting's clients assessed "costs to serve," they discovered something they had only "suspected" for years: that "its number-two revenue producer was, in fact, unprofitable."*

3. Growth potential. Even a low-producing account may be a good candidate for LAMP planning if there are undeveloped opportunities or challenges there that your company can address. To identify such areas of potential growth, leverage

---

*The Seven Keys to Managing Strategic Accounts, p. 68.

the cross-functional insights of an account management team, and think about each account as a "market" in its own right. Don't confine yourself to what you're selling the account right now. Consider the account's total spending on the types of products and services you supply and ask yourself if there are other areas—regions, product lines, distribution channels—that you might investigate to improve your wallet share.

4. Relationship potential. To go beyond transactional selling to true account management, you need to look beyond the numbers for evidence of strategic potential, that is, evidence that this Large Account actually wants to partner with you, and is willing to invest the time and resources that a good partnership requires. We'll go into this in some detail in Chapter 4, where we explain the Buy-Sell Hierarchy. For now, we'll just say, as you're trying to select your "best few" Large Accounts, that you should ideally target those candidates who want a long-term relationship with you just as firmly, and on just as solid grounds, as you want one with them.

Zeroing In: Field of Play

In our corporate workshops, after clients have identified which Large Account they want to set strategies for, we ask them to zero in with greater precision on a *particular* portion of the targeted account that they want to concentrate on. We call this portion of the account the Field of Play. Think of it as a manageable strategic arena.

The Field of Play could be a division, a business unit, or some other segment of the customer's organization. But it has to be a segment as defined by the *customer's* structure. We'll explain in a minute why this is so important. First, let's address a more general question. Why should you focus on a limited, designated Field of Play within your targeted Large Account?

Consider the case of one of our clients—a leading-edge data service company that provides credit information to the financial and insurance industries. One of its most lucrative accounts is American Express; the account brought in nearly eight figures in revenue last year. But "American Express" is not a uniform entity. It's composed of numerous subsidiaries, including (to name a few) Travel Related Services, IDS Financial Services, Shearson Lehman Hutton, and American Express Bank. Each of these subsidiaries is in turn a huge, multi-armed concern employing thousands of people worldwide. TRS alone manages businesses in cards and traveler's checks, data-based services, direct marketing, merchandising, and publishing. Nobody sells— nobody *could* sell—to all these businesses in the same way or with the same account strategy. Trying to do so would be confusing and self-destructive. So when our client targets "the AMEX account," it practices a kind of differential "chunking," setting one strategy for IDS, one for Shearson, and so on. It's *got* to start by asking "Which AMEX?"

Ian Irving, one of our U.K.-based sales consultants, describes the process of zeroing in on Field of Play as it transpired in a recent LAMP workshop. One of the participants had relationships with contacts at a division of Unilever—a multinational with 247,000 employees, regional separate business groups on six continents, and a product portfolio that includes such household brands as Lipton, Hellmann's, Birds Eye, Slim-Fast, and Knorr. In trying to define her Large Account, this rep began by saying, matter-of-factly, "It's Unilever." Irving asked her to narrow that down.

"Fine," I told her. "But Unilever is a multibillion-dollar enterprise with offices in one hundred countries. And this gigantic Unilever universe doesn't pay the bills, right? It doesn't directly supply you with any revenue." She agreed, and so she started to break it down. First she figured that maybe her Large Account within that universe was the Bestfoods division. Then, because she had no contacts in the United States or Asia, she narrowed the Field of Play down to Bestfoods Europe. But even that turned out to be too broad. She knew high-level managers on the customer service side of the business, but nobody on the grocery side— so it looked like the Field of Play was really something like "the customer service function of Bestfoods Europe." That's a very different—and more manageable—customer than giant Unilever. That was a revelation for this rep, and that's what is really so powerful about the Field of Play concept. It helps you understand better what the account really is, so you can start to build an engagement strategy that covers all the key players.

The AMEX and Unilever cases are hardly unique. Most companies today grow by subdividing. Even the ones that say they're sticking to the knitting tend to define knitting in very diversified terms. Johnson & Johnson, for example, is still a health care enterprise, but it now oversees two hundred operating companies and sells literally thousands of different products. In addition to its traditional Band-Aids and baby products, it also delivers—on a global basis—a vast array of pharmaceuticals, as well as such surgical necessities as joint reconstruction prostheses and arterial stents. All of these product lines are handled by separate management structures. In fact, the typical Large Account today resembles what a friend of ours calls a corporate octopus. And in these days of rampant globalization, the arms of that octopus often spread over vast geographies and dozens of P&L centers, making it impossible to set a workable strategy for the whole beast all at once. Sales organizations that try to do that inevitably lose their focus and create fuzzy strategies. That's why this third phase of account selection is not optional.

What are the criteria for selecting a Field of Play? In zeroing in on a manageable portion of an account, we've found that it's helpful to ask yourself the following test questions:

1. *Where are their problems?* In which segment is the account having problems that we may be able to address? What issues are keeping C level managers up at night? Which of our company's core competencies are aligned with those issues? Where are we currently best positioned to understand those problems and to leverage our particular strengths to create solutions? Remember our basic premise: In terms of their bottom line and their customer relationships, in which strategic arena can we produce the biggest payoff or make the biggest contribution?

2. What are our priorities? Which part of the account is really a priority for us? Where could effective account management bring us the best improvement in terms of long-range revenue (ROI) and "return on relationship investment" (RORI)? We've urged you to target an account where something is "off." We *don't* mean the billion-dollar pie-in-the-sky customer where you barely have a foot in the door. We're not saying you shouldn't think about improving low-performing accounts. But in setting LAMP strategies, start with the winners—with those pieces of already good business that more effective account management could make even better. Choose a Field of Play that will build on the priorities you're already realizing.

3. What's the account's potential? We've stressed not biting off more than you can chew. Don't bite off too little either. Think about whether you could be positioned with a broader segment of the account. For example, if you now sell to only one of the Geoplex Company's ten divisions, is it feasible that you could reach all those in North America or all those in Europe? Can you move from a single business unit to a division, from a division to a group? Think about where your Field of Play might be broadened over the next few years. Where, finally, is there the greatest untapped potential for both of your companies to profit by an ongoing relationship?

4. What's our knowledge base? In which part of the Large Account do we have the most knowledge or the best knowledge? How much do we currently understand about the internal organization of the account? About the account's problems, threats, and opportunities? About trends in the industry of which it's a part? We'll spend most of Part II of this book showing how detailed Situation Appraisal can bring you answers to these questions. But if you don't have some preliminary handle on them now, you're probably not looking at a feasible Field of Play.

5. *How does the account see itself?* This last criterion is as critical as it is often neglected. In determining whether or not this final selection phase is really getting you to a manageable Field of Play, ask yourself: Does this Field of Play relate to *how the customer sees itself?*

This last question is critical because the way the customer wants to buy may or may not correlate with the way you want to sell, the way your sales and marketing people operate, or the depth of relationship you'd like to develop. It's traditional for sales organizations to be self-centered, and thus to segment corporate customers according to their own territorial divisions. In B2B engagements, that often backfires. Consider the case of the European company that intended to build business with a major U.S. firm by developing a great relationship with its New York headquarters. That strategy worked fine on the East Coast, but not at all for the West Coast division, which was organized independently and made decisions accordingly. This is a great example of how an imperfect understanding of the *customer's perceptions* can lead to fuzzy strategizing and lost sales. And it's common in most sales organizations.

Two Complications

As critical as it is to define your Field of Play accurately, we're not suggesting that this is an easy process. As the example of Ian Irving's would-be "Unilever" rep indicates, even veteran salespeople sometimes have to devote considerable effort to zeroing in from Large Account to Field of Play. In many cases, moreover, the process is complicated not only by the unwieldiness of corporate structures but by two additional elements.

Compensation conflicts. First, while your account team may have successfully defined a Field of Play—and identified an immediate relational or revenue goal within that Field of Play—other teams or other structures in your organization may not share the same incentives to achieve those goals as your team members do. Their initiatives in the same Large Account may not coincide with yours. Indeed, in some cases they may overlap with or even contradict yours. This confusion is typically the result of the selling organization's compensation structures, which may have nothing to do with how the Large Account—or any of its various Fields of Play—wants to buy. One of our veteran LAMP instructors explains:

> Say you're a Northeast sales rep for a large health products firm, and to make your quota you have to place ten cardiac monitors in a certain Connecticut hospital. But at the same time, your company is working a corporate deal with that hospital's regional management, planning to place two hundred monitors, across five affiliated hospitals, in the same quarter. If the corporate deal flies, you won't make your number, and on top of that your account contacts are going to be mad because they've lost control of a purchase that you told them was their decision. It's a common scenario, and not just in health care. Whenever you have three or four or twenty different reps calling on the same account, and they're all compensated differently, you're going to encounter conflicts among Fields of Play.

People do what you pay them to do. So if your compensation structures aren't aligned—in fact, if they're not aligned according to how the customer wants to buy—you're going to encounter conflicts like this one, and even if you don't lose business, you may alienate team members. The solution lies in better team organization—something we'll be addressing frequently throughout this book.

Moving targets. The second problem relates to the dynamism of the economic environment—and especially to the volatile nature of organizational structure. The challenging fact is that the company you sell to today may be, in terms of effective relational strategy, an entirely different company next month. Both internally (in terms of firings, hirings, and reorganizations) and externally (in terms of centralization and decentralization, mergers and acquisitions), corporate accounts morph frequently. Effective Large Account strategy takes that reality to heart. You have to redefine your Field of Play according to circumstances—meaning the circumstances in the customer's field of vision. If a company is bought or undergoes an internal restructuring that alters the way your contacts perceive themselves, you may be suddenly dealing with an entirely different Field of Play.

And you can't count on the customer's org chart to set you straight. Even if the customer doesn't go through a reorganization per se, many other less visible factors may still impact the way that decisions are made. Maybe there's a new consultant who has the CEO's ear. Maybe a German subsidiary has discovered a new best practice, and suddenly everyone in Chicago is saying "We'll do that, too." This is why constant review of the customer's situation is so essential.

Field of Play depends entirely on how the account sees itself, and on how it wants to deal with you. You've got to keep that under a microscope, in every customer contact. Field of Play isn't a section of the org chart. It's a moving target.

In fact, much the same comment can be made about LAMP strategy overall. In the next section of the book, we'll start explaining the individual components of that strategy and showing how, in this incredibly fast-moving economy, constant reassessment is a key to growing healthy relationships.

CHAPTER 3

A Real-World Example

"Theory is very fine, but facts pay the rent."

—Alexander Yarrowville

IN THIS CHAPTER, IN ORDER TO MAKE THE LAMP PRINCIPLES WE'VE JUST discussed concrete and visible, we introduce an illustrative case study. Although the names of the companies and individuals involved are fictionalized, the example itself is real. It's based on the experiences of Miller Heiman clients who have encountered similar scenarios and utilized similar strategies to manage their Large Account relationships.

The story of how "PreComm, Inc." manages its relationship with "Datavoc PLC" is therefore neither unique nor unusual. It reflects the challenges that businesses large and small are facing today, and it demonstrates practically just how valuable LAMP can be in meeting those challenges. We begin the story here, and we'll return to it periodically throughout the book.

The Background

Precision Communications, Inc., commonly known as PreComm, is a mid-sized firm that supplies a wide range of communications expertise to the manufacturing sector. As a designer of ICs (integrated circuits), it supplies many of the internal controllers and ICs needed for high-tech, domestic, and industrial appliances to communicate with hosts or each other as well as the "know-how" to enable them. Although its main research, design, and manufacturing operations are based in the United States, PreComm is a global operation. It manufactures in Europe and also has a production line in the Far East. Its technical experts and consultants are all regionally based, and it also maintains sales forces in the U.S., Europe, Latin America, and Asia. Recently it has been viewing the vast Chinese market with growing enthusiasm. Employing about six hundred people, the privately owned company did $400 million in sales last year. In an increasingly competitive market, it is striving to grow that revenue by living up to a recently coined corporate slogan: "Communication Excellence Through Innovation and Design."

Roughly one-fifth of PreComm's revenue stream comes from its single biggest customer, the London-based, internationally known communications and engineering company Datavoc PLC. Although Datavoc's main market is in selling environmental control, telephone, and communications systems business-to-business, it has achieved household-name status from its home appliance lines. One in every five U.K. homes, and one in every eight German ones, has a Datavoc phone or heating system, while tens of thousands of residential customers around the globe own Datavoc heating or air-conditioning systems or microwave ovens. The firm boasts blue-chip status on the London stock exchange, employs 26,000 people, and manages a multimillion-pound procurement budget to secure the many components its products require. For components that it produces, PreComm has a 35 percent "wallet share" of that budget.

Datavoc is definitely a Large Account that PreComm doesn't want to lose. But recent developments have begun to threaten the account's stability. Pressures from environmentalists, safety watchdogs, and industrial insurers are increasing Datavoc's manufacturing costs even as its markets are being attacked by established competitors and Asian newcomers. To meet this dual challenge, Datavoc's President, Martin Chaucer, has mandated a procurement centralization initiative called Global

Commodity Sourcing. He has also directed the company's six plant managers to look more closely at Chinese vendors and to further investigate the potential of manufacturing there. The same country that looks like a new market to PreComm appeals to Datavoc as a potential source of lower-cost components and manufacturing. And, in a recent shareholder report, Chaucer has promised to improve the branding and time-to-market of Datavoc products without incurring any damage to the company's cost base.

What all of this means to PreComm is that a major source of its revenue is becoming uncertain—a scenario in which being "pushed down to commodity" is a real threat. The threat is all the more disturbing because the recent history of the two companies has been fraught with tension. Datavoc engineers have long appreciated the superior quality of PreComm products, but their counterparts in procurement have negotiated strictly on price. Up until about a year ago, they even went so far as to accept the engineers' recommendations for PreComm designs—offered through a partnership called Design Innovation—and then hawk the design around to competing suppliers. PreComm responded by withdrawing the partnership, which cost them several months in the vendor wilderness. They only regained a foothold in the Datavoc account when they introduced a new line of wireless control units, but delivering this product, too, has only revived the old debate: Datavoc's engineers love the technical advantage and flexibility it brings, but procurement still wants it cheaper.

Amidst all of this tension, nobody is talking much about the consumer—the end user who suffers directly from unreliable components and failures. Yet, if Chaucer is taking his branding mandate seriously, this might be exactly the area in which PreComm can get some traction.

Identifying the Field of Play—And Forming a Team

Pat Murphy, a PreComm field rep based in London, has been charged by his manager, Sam Jones, to devise a strategy for increasing the company's wallet share with Datavoc—or at least preventing the revenue loss that a policy of business-as-usual will almost certainly lead to. Since he's been trained in LAMP, Murphy knows that his first order of business in drafting such a strategy is to identify *which* Datavoc he and Jones want to target. That is, he needs to identify the Field of Play.

Reviewing his experiences in the two years he's been working with the international company, Murphy quickly realizes that his base of contacts at Datavoc is both operationally and geographically localized. Virtually everybody he knows works for the European Manufacturing division—that has been the sole point of contact and the sole source of transactions. Neither he nor Jones knows anyone in sales, finance, or any other Datavoc operating function. Nor do they know anyone in manufacturing outside Europe.

This fact makes the identification of the Field of Play fairly straightforward. Murphy isn't going to waste time drafting an amorphous and largely irrelevant "Datavoc strategy." Instead, he'll home in on the area where he's already positioned: "Datavoc's European Manufacturing division." This doesn't mean that PreComm may not also do business with Datavoc's other divisions. But those groups will be the province of other account managers. For Murphy's group, European Manufacturing is the Field of Play.

Having specified the Field of Play, Murphy's next step is to identify the most appropriate people to have on his team—the PreComm professionals who can most effectively help him build an engagement strategy that covers all the key players. Murphy decides that, in addition to himself, the team should have the following three members:

- *Sam Jones*, his manager, who has overseen the Datavoc account for the past several years—and who is painfully aware of PreComm's precarious position;
- *David Olsen*, a design engineer, who can interface with Datavoc's engineers and provide technical expertise as well as credibility; and

- *Robert Glock*, the company's recently promoted Regional
  VP for Europe and thus a potentially influential executive
  bargaining voice.

Murphy contacts each of these people, explains why keeping the Datavoc relationship positive is essential to PreComm's
continued financial health, and establishes a multiple-contact
Web address in his e-mail functionality. There's just one more
thing to do before he schedules an initial planning session.

Getting Executive Sign-off

Murphy knows that, without the ability to marshal internal
resources quickly in response to the Field of Play's evolving
needs, any plan the team creates will be doomed to failure. To
guard against that, he needs—if not actually on his team, at least
on his side—an executive who appreciates the importance of
this particular Large Account, and who has the clout (and
the sign-off authority) to "liberate" unbudgeted resources if
and when the need arises. So he makes one more call, to
the PreComm Vice President of Finance, Alicia Carvounis, in
the U.S.

As the company's chief numbers cruncher, Carvounis is well
positioned to understand both Datavoc's cost-control issues
and the disaster it could be for her company if they took their
business elsewhere. Murphy has met her a couple of times, once
on a trip to the head office and again when she visited London,
and has found her to be an articulate and vocal champion of relationship building. Unlike many finance people, she also understands the truth of the old adage "You've got to spend
money to make money." And she reports directly to the company CEO, William Langland. So she looks like an ideal choice
for sponsoring executive.

Once she hears Murphy's description of the Datavoc scenario, Carvounis agrees that this is an account PreComm can't
afford to lose. And she pledges her personal support—including
conference call participation, if need be—for the Large Account

strategy Murphy will be putting together. Murphy is of course delighted. To have an executive of Carvounis's stature on his team—even on an ad hoc basis—is an organizational plus. Her presence will lend credibility to the team's efforts, and it will minimize the danger of their plan falling through because it is insufficiently supported at the corporate level.

With Carvounis on board, Murphy is confident that he has formed a viable team. So he turns to the next step in the LAMP planning process, Situation Appraisal. We turn to that step as well, in Part II.

PART II

Situation Appraisal

CHAPTER 4

The Buy-Sell Hierarchy

"The higher up the food chain you get, the more specific, thoughtful, and tailor-made your discussions and your ideas need to be."

—Patrick Thomas,
Development Director for Global and Strategic Accounts,
Aon Risk Services International

BEFORE YOU CAN BEGIN TO SET A LARGE ACCOUNT STRATEGY, YOU HAVE to determine where you stand, right now, with the account. This sounds like common sense, yet every day, so-called strategies lead nowhere because account teams have failed to dedicate themselves seriously to this critical first step. Assuming the best rather than investigating their current position with the account, they develop a false sense of reality and end up like bewildered trailblazers lost in the woods, wondering why their exquisitely detailed maps will not reveal their coordinates.

The basis of every good strategy is accurate information—and that information must begin with an assessment of your *position*. That is why we begin this section on Situation Appraisal by introducing the concept of the Buy-Sell Hierarchy. Our uniquely field-tested model for assessing Large Account position, it provides reliable benchmarks to measure not only how you see the account but—far more importantly—how the account, right now, sees you and your company.

As you can see from the diagram that follows, what we call the Buy-Sell Hierarchy of possible business relationships is divided into five levels. We'll describe each of these levels in detail. But let's start with some general observations.

First, it's not you, but your *customers*, that is, the key individuals in your Field of Play, who decide at what level of the hierarchy you're positioned—and each of them may have a different view of the matter. There's some irony here. We'll be recommending that you "work your way up" the Buy-Sell Hierarchy; yet it's the individuals you work with in the account who decide how successfully you do this. You've got to *earn the right* to be perceived as an "upper-level" supplier. That's why the descriptions at each level of the hierarchy refer to the Field of Play's assessment of your company's position.

Second, although in the diagram the levels of the Buy-Sell Hierarchy look like steps, it's really more accurate to think of them as positions along a continuum. Your customers will probably have a pretty solid sense of where you're positioned—that is, of where they see you on the hierarchy—but it may not be quantifiable: No magic signal will inform you that in the customer's

BUY-SELL HIERARCHY

eyes you've just moved from Level 2 to Level 3. That will become evident through the way you operate together, not from any official passing of a barrier.

Third, the hierarchy isn't as stable as it looks in this static diagram. One of our colleagues likes to compare the Buy-Sell Hierarchy to a moving stairway, or escalator—one that moves, sometimes unpredictably, in both directions. Which means that, even though you may be positioned at Level 3 today, unless you're vigilant you may find yourself at Level 2 tomorrow.

We'll explain the other material in the hierarchy diagram as we move through the chapter. Let's start by looking more closely at the bottom level.

Level 1: The Commodity Corner

At the first, and lowest, level of business relationship, you are seen as the supplier of a commodity. It's easy to get positioned at this level, but there's seldom much leverage here for establishing long-term relationships. Here's why.

In the New York and Chicago futures markets, a commodity is something traded in bulk, with no regard for special features or added value. Oats, gold, crude oil, gypsum, pork bellies: These very different products have one thing in common. They have to meet minimum standards, but beyond those standards there's virtually no competition with regard to quality. One supplier's East Texas crude is pretty much the same as the next supplier's. One producer's 24 karat gold is indistinguishable from that of the competition. Availability and (most important) price are the only differentiators among suppliers of commodities.

You don't need to be a futures trader to be seen as the supplier of a mere "commodity." You can provide computer workstations to insurance companies, but if Metropolitan Life thinks your systems are exactly the same as everyone else's, it doesn't matter whether they "really" are or not. It's the inability of the customer to differentiate that defines a product or service as a commodity. When there's no perceived difference, and all vendors meet the required minimum specifications, you might as well be pushing gold or crude oil.

There's nothing wrong with that, if that's what you want to do. But in targeting Large Accounts, it's usually a precarious position. When customers see you as a commodity supplier, you have virtually no control over what happens in their accounts, and almost no chance of growing a long-term relationship. Why? Because commodity trading has very simple rules: "Buy cheap, sell dear." If your customers see what you provide as indistinguishable from what your competitors can provide—if you're merely pushing a product rather than developing a relationship—then your only bargaining chips are availability and low price. Not a very secure position.

Yet, in a world that's driven by supply chain economies, it's a distressingly common one. As we pointed out in Chapter 1, the purchasing function in many companies today has become an engine for narrowing the supplier base, and for pushing the short list of approved vendors into commodity status. Some large trucking firms today, for example, circumvent the sales function entirely when they buy tires; they just put out an order on the Internet and take the lowest bid. This process is also common in other automotive segments, where electronically enabled bidding can put tremendous pressure on suppliers.

For example, one of our clients supplies exhaust and emissions control products to major automobile manufacturers. One of its largest accounts, a Big Three manufacturer, has recently adopted auction-based sourcing, obliging our client and its competitors to vie for contracts through an Internet bidding protocol that is deliberately structured to push them toward commodity, whether they're bidding on individual parts or complex emission systems. Miller Heiman Sales Consultant Mark Sellers explains how it works.

"Our client is in a private room, viewing the auction on two screens," he says. "One shows a spreadsheet of their bids—including piece part information, margin information, sales price, and so on—as well as their overall bid number, which changes in real time as competing suppliers bid from *their* private rooms. The other screen shows a real-time ranking of the suppliers and their bids, but without identifying them by name. So they all know where they stand, but they don't know whom they're up against. As a result, they get an incomplete picture of the competitive landscape." Obviously, this is a system that works against—and in fact is designed to work against—the supplier, by giving the manufacturer access to much fuller information.

"Because of the limited visibility," says Sellers, "even though the manufacturer doesn't always go with the lowest bid, there's a built-in pressure to bid low just to stay in the game. Winning suppliers might easily find that they've bid lower than they needed to. The whole structure allows the manufacturer to weed out some suppliers entirely and put incredible price pressure on the rest."

Internet auctions, the corporate version of eBay, are probably the most blatant example of the push to commoditization, but they're not the only one. "As we aspire to developing good relationships with our customers," says Experian's Sales Director Neville Seabridge, "we are faced more and more with the professional buyer. And their entire function seems to be to discredit your importance, to push you—whatever your aspirations—into a commodity corner."

This can't be laid entirely at the purchaser's door. In fact, some vendors' reps actually invite being pushed into that corner, because it's easier to secure yourself as a "good enough" supplier than to make the extra effort to differentiate yourself and move up the hierarchy. In addition, it's quite possible, as a friend of ours puts it, to "make a boatload of money" by being positioned as a reliable, low-price vendor. The problem is that the relationships that you can build at this level generally rest on "friendship" (or price alone) and are *not* secure. A friend of ours calls them "veneer" relationships: "They're based on a very thin veneer of knowledge about the customer, and are therefore focused entirely on products," he says. "When salespeople like this get stuck at the commodity level, it isn't necessarily because their clients don't want them to move up, but because they're afraid to leave their own pink blanket comfort zones."

Often, people who get stuck—willingly or not—at Level 1 try to convince themselves that it's not a failure to establish differentiation but the product itself that keeps them there. When the product is a commodity, they reason, there's no way it can be positioned as something else. That may sound logical, but it's not. In fact, your position on the Buy-Sell Hierarchy has little to do with your product or service. There's little to no difference between the major cola drinks, for example, in terms of "product specs," yet they are differentiated markedly, in the consumer and B2B markets, based on how their Large Accounts perceive them.

Ask yourself why one company, Morton, sells half of all the table salt in the United States. It's not because their NaCl is different from everyone else's. It's because Morton has invested wisely in creating a perception—in their case, a consumer perception—that positions them in their customers' (the retailers') eyes as something more than a salt vendor. Morton creates consumer demand, which translates to the retailers as faster stock turnover, increased revenue, and more satisfied customers. Those advantages translate into a relationship that goes way beyond salt.

Or consider Ethicon, a multimillion-dollar business in the Johnson & Johnson family of companies whose principal product line is surgical sutures. Sutures are pretty close to being a commodity item, yet Ethicon has established close and durable relationships with many of its hospital customers. How? By bringing them such added values as marketing assistance and technical training. Those contributions help to position Ethicon way up the Buy-Sell Hierarchy with selected accounts, despite the fact that their products in themselves provide little differentiation.

Level 2: Providing "Good" Products

On the second level of the hierarchy, your customer sees you as the supplier of "good" products or services—products, for example, that incorporate state-of-the-art technology, or that meet more than usually exacting technical specifications, or that are backed up by great service and support. Not just a minimally acceptable computer, but one that's extremely fast or user-friendly. Not just an overnight courier service, but one that offers next-day 10:00 A.M. delivery and universal brand recognition. Not just a 24/7 help line, but one that is staffed by exceptionally courteous and skillful technicians.

Any product or service feature that sets you apart from the competition, that gets you recognized by your customers as an innovator, can help you establish second-level business relationships. Obviously this is an improvement. But to be seen as providing "good product" is still a tenuous relationship position.

The reason is simple: competition. You can *establish* a competitive position with bells and whistles (or faster service or other add-ons), but you can't *maintain* it. Unless you've got a patent lock on your distinctive feature or benefit—these days, even when you do—eventually the competition not only catches up but leapfrogs over you, and you're back to selling commodity-style again, with the "distinctive" features now part of everybody's arsenal. This happens most blatantly in telecommunications. One mobile phone company introduces a color screen or a silent ring or a picture-messaging feature that immediately puts it ahead of the pack. Six months later, after everybody from Tokyo to Tucson has copied it, it's part of the new minimum standards, and the battle goes on, cranked up another notch.

One of our clients is a large trucking firm. The president of that company joked with us a couple of years ago about the limitations of good-product positioning. With ten or twelve hungry competitors on his tail, he said, it was no longer sufficient just to "give good truck." "All the major players now give good truck. Clean, well-maintained vehicles. On-time pickup and delivery. Courteous drivers. Guarantees against breakage. All of that has now become the norm. If you want to play in this league, you have to give more and better service on top of that."

This is a good description of the advantages—and limitations—of delivering a "better" product. Let's look now at what our friend meant by "more."

Level 3: Dedicated Service

At the third level of the Buy-Sell Hierarchy, you've earned the right to be seen not just as the provider of excellent products, services, or solutions, but as a company that makes a special effort on the customer's behalf. What gets you to Level 3 is the Field of Play's understanding that it's getting something *more* than your other customers are getting. At Level 2 you install bug-free computer systems on time, for all your customers; at Level 3, you provide a system training program that is tailored to a specific customer's skill sets. At Level 2 you provide everyone with round-the-clock tech support; at Level 3, you give one Field of Play a dedicated help line.

To clarify the difference between Level 2 and Level 3 service, consider one of the world's great service companies, Enterprise Rent-A-Car. "They've got a mom-and-pop feel to them," says one colleague who uses them routinely, "but their customer service is absolutely world-class. They'll pick you up, they're on top of your reservation, they follow up if you have any questions—this is a company that really treats you as if you matter." That's a commonly heard accolade about Enterprise, but precisely because it's so common, you can tell that what it's describing is a Level 2 perception. Enterprise has built a world-class service reputation by treating all of its customers in this "service counts" fashion.

But suppose your company is a faithful Enterprise customer and, to encourage your continued support, the rental firm offers your company free vehicle upgrades or simplified billing to match your account practices or complimentary service for your CEO. In this situation, it's likely that your company's perception of the Enterprise relationship would change: You would see them as a supplier that goes "above and beyond" in serving you. And they would have moved, in your eyes, from a Level 2 to a Level 3 relationship.

Or take FedEx. It leads the pack in overnight package delivery not because it gets your letter there on time—that's a Level 1 accomplishment that all carriers have to deliver just to stay in business. For many of its customers—especially its small, individual customers—FedEx is probably perceived at Level 2: It dominates the overnight letter market because it provides everyone such "extras" as computer tracking, a vast network of accessible drop-off points, computerized memory of customer preferences, and consistent, professional service at every stop along the way. But if FedEx values your account enough to offer you something beyond this great service menu—say, additional delivery attempts if you're not in, or free consultation services—they may be able to develop a Level 3 relationship with your company. Again, it's not the service itself that gets a provider to Level 3, but the fact that the service helps build a differentiated relationship with a specific Field of Play.

Level 4: Crossing the Chasm to Business Issues

At the first three levels of relationship, the number of competitors remains high. So does your customer's sensitivity to product price. But both of those things change dramatically when you make the leap to the fourth level of the hierarchy. And that leap is *major*. To call it "crossing the chasm" is not an understatement.

On the fourth level, customers perceive your company as providing not just good products and extra service, but help in the understanding of their business issues. When you're positioned here, you understand each account's business problems and objectives almost as well as you do your own. You generate ideas for addressing not just customers' day-to-day operational needs but their ongoing concerns about things like profit, productivity, and go-to-market strategies. You may provide not just products and services that address those concerns, but a wide range of ancillary supports that may have virtually nothing to do with your product or service.

Example: Suppose you sell information systems to a manufacturer who is concerned about getting an inventory problem under control. One of your mid-range systems would solve the problem quickly, efficiently, and at reasonable cost. She'd probably buy a more expensive, top-of-the-line configuration, though. It's loaded with features she will never use, but it would double your revenue from that account and the salesperson's commission. Which system do you sell her?

If you're thinking long-term, there's no contest. You leave the sell-it-and-run approach to companies that see their customers as easy targets, and you deliver the system that will best meet *the customer's* business needs. And you do it for the most pragmatic of reasons: It will help you build a relationship of trust and mutual value that, over time, will make both of your organizations more profitable. Customers who see you saving them money are going to seek you out beyond this quota period: Because you've earned the right to be perceived as a partner, they'll want your business as much as you want theirs.

And they will want it *even if it costs them a little more*. As you cross the chasm into a Level 4 relationship, you're contributing something that few competitors even think about providing, and you can begin to sell up to value, not down to price. This doesn't mean that, as you move up the hierarchy, you can simply jack up your prices or refuse to discount. It means that your conversations with the account are less likely to be price-sensitive, because you're perceived as delivering value that includes your product and service offerings but goes beyond them. Paying for that type of value shows enlightened self-interest. Show me how to lower my costs, increase my productivity, or boost my profit, and of course I'm going to want to do business with your company. Not just for this quarter, but for the long run. That's what sustaining a value-added relationship is all about.

Delivering bottom-line value, however, will get you positioned as a Level 4 supplier only if people in the Large Account see a clear and explicit *connection* between your contribution and the added value to their firm. Here, as in account relationships generally, what counts is the customer's perception—which is something that you often have to work at sharpening. This is why the organizations that most successfully manage high-level relationships invest considerable energy in "merchandising" their successes—in showing key account players, in every instance, how their business concerns have been directly impacted by the supplier's activities.

Here's an example of how to do it right. A British trade organization recently decided that it wanted to offer its members preferential rates on life insurance. It broached the idea to its insurance company, and since the insurer considered the trade body an important Large Account, it used the opportunity to significantly improve its position on the Buy-Sell Hierarchy. First, as well as providing the trade body with the requested rates, it also proposed some additional product features (like free coverage for members' children) that placed them immediately at Level 2 of the hierarchy—as a provider of more-than-commodity products and services. Then, without being asked, the insurer provided the trade organization with access to a free phone line staffed by a team dedicated to the account and its members. That "extra," for this account alone, brought the insurer (in the customer's eyes) to Level 3.

The leap to Level 4 came when the trade body informed the insurer that they had some concerns about how to market the new offering to their members and still maintain acceptable margins. That was a business, or Level 4, issue—and to help the trade body meet it, the insurer immediately assigned a marketing expert to the account. She provided market intelligence that helped the trade body reach its members more effectively, and as a result the new offering was a rapid success. After eighteen months, the insurer raised its prices, with the full consent of the account, which also increased its margins—and its ongoing business with the insurer. This steady progress from Level 2 to Level 4 was made possible by the insurer's willingness to go beyond product, and to help the Large Account be a more profitable business. This is a good example of the commitment required at upper levels of the hierarchy, and of the rewards that can be realized by companies willing to make it.

Why the Chasm Exists

Of course it doesn't always work out this way. We've said that moving up from Level 3 to Level 4 is like crossing a chasm. There are several reasons why making this move is so difficult.

First is organizations' natural tendency to send their field people out in "selling mode," intent chiefly on meeting quotas and pushing product. This is a time-honored pattern that, in today's relationship-anchored world, is becoming increasingly self-destructive. Of course you have to make transactions in order to survive. But in Large Account management, transactions must be the secondary effect of maintaining the relationship. If your prime reason for meeting a customer is to sell him something, he will know that, and your chances of building a relationship (the source, remember, of multiple transactions) will be severely limited. If you're in "product push mode," therefore, you cannot bridge the chasm.

A second, related reason is the fact that, however much lip service they may pay to helping their customers become more profitable, most suppliers know very little about their customers' businesses. In fact, a benchmarking study done by the HR Chally Group found that, when companies were asked to identify areas where their suppliers might improve their selling efforts, the most common response was "increased competency in understanding our business."* Because the point of managing an external asset is to improve it as a business, fail-

---

World Class Sales Excellence 10 Year Research Report (HR Chally Group, 2002), p. 29.

ing to become as well versed in your customer's business as you are in your own is a sure way to put that asset at risk. And that is exactly the situation most "account managers" are in. They cannot communicate at Level 4 or Level 5 because, unlike the British insurer we've just described, they don't understand the customer's language.

A third reason is intimidation. To develop effective relationships at the top of the hierarchy, you have to be able to communicate with senior management—and that is something that makes all but the most seasoned reps uneasy. This is why you have to perform a careful assessment of a Large Account's many key players—and be sure that every one of them is covered. This isn't easy. It's much more comfortable to deal with the people you know, even if they're low-level people, and to keep your eye on the radar screen that's familiar. The trouble is, you cannot work your way up the hierarchy while you're standing at that screen. To be at Level 4, you must not only become expert in your customer's business; someone on your team must also be able to communicate that expertise, and thereby build relationships, at executive levels.

Fourth is expense—or perceived expense. Building good business relationships costs money, time, and resources. Some companies would prefer not to make that commitment. And in some cases that may be wise. Even though being highly positioned decreases the importance of price and competition, this doesn't mean you want—or can afford to support—this position with every account. Indeed, part of what a good LAMP strategy does is help you define which accounts are worth the "full treatment," and which ones can be better managed at a lower level of commitment. It's fine to be in a Level 1 or 2 or 3 position, if it's providing the results you want—high-volume sales, for example, or good margins. But you shouldn't settle for being in these positions if you'd prefer to go higher.

Last, the Large Account itself may not want you to cross the chasm. Wal-Mart, for example, is well known for buying on price. Even with its oldest and most reliable suppliers, its corporate strategy is to favor low bids, and to support consultative relationships only to the extent that they enhance their discounting advantage. If you're working with that type of customer, you're not getting across the chasm. On the other hand, some companies that are perceived as being tough on price may, in fact, be quite interested in developing a relationship. For example, a major pharmaceutical company we work with once ran a LAMP program "in reverse" to establish better lines of communication with five of its principal suppliers; it was inviting those vendors, in effect, to cross the chasm.

Level 5: Becoming the Account's "External Asset"

In the HR Chally benchmarking study that we just cited, you'll recall, researchers found that customers' single most common complaint was that the suppliers who wanted their business *did not understand their business problems*. Most suppliers were locked into "product-selling mode," when what their customers wanted was expert consultation. If you can provide that kind of consultation—and only if you can provide it—you've got a shot at reaching the top of the Buy-Sell Hierarchy, Level 5. The differentiation you achieve at this level can be extraordinary.

We've explained why it's important to think of your Large Accounts as "external assets"—critical elements to your organization's sustainability. In a truly mutual business relationship, this cuts both ways. Just as your Large Accounts provide essential fuel for your company, you do the same for them. *And they see it this way.* When a Large Account perceives you as a Level 5 player, you are considered their external asset—and are taken just as seriously as if you were actually on their payroll. At Level 5, you've become an ex officio member—in some companies even an official member—of the customer's team. You're no longer a competing vendor, but a trusted advisor. People in the account stop thinking about what kind of discounts they can shoehorn you into when they're seeking your advice and counsel for running the ship.

In this best of all business relationships, you go beyond providing your customers with good products or exceptional service, and even beyond giving them help with short-term business concerns. As a consulting partner rather than a mere provider, you contribute to their ongoing organizational productivity, and are therefore rightly perceived—by people up and down the scale of their organization—as helping them run their business. When it comes to "unfair competitive advantage," this is as good as it gets.

How does this work? Suppose, for example, that one of your Large Accounts wants to shore up a faltering profit margin, and its strategy is to decentralize operations, allowing division managers greater control over their profit centers. In this scenario, any company that helped them breathe life into the account's profit-and-loss statement would be seen as contributing to business issues—Level 4 issues. That's good. But even better would be a company that was seen as helping them both in improving its profit *and* in facilitating the planned decentralization. That kind of contribution would tie into the firm's concerns at both the market and the internal levels—for any company struggling with margins, an ideal combination.

Achieving that combination isn't easy, and in fact even among companies that actively seek this kind of high-level alliance building, few are able to sustain Level 5 relationships with more than a handful of customers. Partly this is a function of limited resources—joint ventures are expensive, after all—and for that reason firms that seek to build such specialized relationships carefully qualify prospective partners before investing. Before committing to a "global" arrangement, for example, industry leaders Marriott, PricewaterhouseCoopers, and IBM routinely assess the potential value of their prospective partners against their own ability to exploit that value to mutual benefit. What do they look for? In the words of one study of global account managers, they seek "the potential for creating value that goes far beyond an increase in product sales, or even share of wallet, to address ways of creating joint value within the relationship."* Only a limited number of accounts can deliver on that criterion.

Room at the Top: The Advantages

In spite of the leverage that you can exert from the top of the hierarchy, few companies ever get there—or even try to. Tradition and intimidation keep all but the most determined and innovative players from trying to do more than deliver great service. They remain in that pink blanket comfort zone, on the near side of the chasm. As a result, there is always room at the top. And aside from the exceptions we've noted of companies who choose to maintain a transactional relationship, the top is generally the place to be. The two-directional arrows at either side of the Buy-Sell Hierarchy diagram indicate why this is so.

First, as you move up in the hierarchy, *competition* decreases, simply because so few companies know how to present themselves as addressing their Large Accounts' organizational and business concerns. Every business in the world pushes its products, while only a few are in competition to sell buyers real solutions for *their* problems. There's plenty of lip service to that effect, but little action.

Second, there's less sensitivity about *price*. If you are recognized by key players in the account as offering not merely good products and services but true added value—value added to the account's business—they will not want to jeopardize that value by shaving percentage points from the price. When you impact the cost equation so that customers see they're not comparing like with like, you become free to some extent from price-point competition. This doesn't necessarily mean you can charge double what your competitor does. It means that if you've improved the return that a customer gets from doing

---

*Nick Speare and Kevin Wilson, with Sam Reese, *Successful Global Account Management* (London: Kogan Page, 2002), p. 30.

business with you, individual transaction price is less likely to be an issue.

Last, the importance of *features* decreases, because the contribution you're seen as making to your clients' businesses outweighs the significance of anybody's bells and whistles. So you're less likely to have to "cram product" and more likely to be delivering solutions rather than promises.

As the legend above the right-hand arrow indicates, the upper-hierarchy approach to account management means being perceived as providing solutions or improving results. Both are defined from the account's point of view. You've got to aim for solutions to each customer's specific, bottom-line problems. The happy irony, of course, is that making such apparently altruistic contributions to a customer's business is also the best way to improve your own.

The Price of Security—Vigilance

We've emphasized the importance of moving up the Buy-Sell Hierarchy. If you're not constantly alert, you can also move down.

If you do this deliberately, that's fine. As we've said, not every account deserves, or can be supported by, the kind of dedication that a Level 4 or Level 5 relationship requires. Markets and opportunities also change over time—sometimes rapidly. So it's perfectly possible to develop a solid, high-level relationship with a company and then decide, because of any number of reasons, that the resources you're devoting to that account would be better applied elsewhere. In this case you might want to agree with the account to do a Stop Investment, and ease your way down the Buy-Sell Hierarchy, where your responsibilities to the account would be less burdensome. (We'll discuss Stop Investments in Part III.)

In most cases where a company moves down the hierarchy, though, this isn't the scenario. Remember our comparison of the Buy-Sell Hierarchy to a moving stairway—one whose natural tendency is to "push you to commodity." Usually, a company that moves down does so unwillingly, for a variety of reasons. Perhaps the account team has developed only a single contact in the account, and that person moves. Perhaps they have been focusing too low in the organization, where upper-level concerns get insufficient attention. Perhaps a competitor has derailed the relationship with something more attractive. And perhaps somebody simply hasn't been paying attention.

This happened once to a friend of ours who was field representative for an industrial components manufacturer. She had fought hard for a foothold with a major account's manager of operations and had positioned herself well by addressing his inventory concerns. Then, after she was "established," she got sidetracked by other business and neglected him for several weeks. It wasn't long—just long enough for his inventory problem to spin out of control. Because the absent are always wrong, he blamed her. When she finally showed up at his door weeks later, she had already tumbled down the hierarchy without knowing it. "He was barely civil to me," she recalls. "It took me three months to regain his trust, show him I hadn't actually caused his problem, and get myself out of the commodity trap."

The moral of this story isn't that you should make more frequent sales calls. That happened to have been true in this case, but it's not a general rule. The real problem was that the rep had built her whole account "strategy" on a single contact, and had failed to manage the multiple interfaces between the account and her company. When she lost her single contact's trust, she had no one else to turn to for support in the account.

We've seen it happen time and again. A strong, competitive company builds a reputation by providing solutions, by speaking to its customer's business and organization issues, by cooperating with key players and top management. But once it's perceived as a real contributor, it can get cocky, then lazy. Believing that its company's position is secure, management starts to take the customer for granted, and to think of the account as a sure thing. Next stop: churn.

The only way to avoid this common problem is to remember that it's your customers, not you, who place you at a given level of the Buy-Sell Hierarchy—and that the position of each contact you develop in the Large Account dictates the maximum level you can reach on the hierarchy. If the people you interface with are only concerned with Level 2 and Level 3 product-related issues, no amount of discipline is going to magically get you to Level 4, where the primary concern is business issues. Furthermore, even if you're interfacing at the higher levels, you can still find yourself tumbling down the escalator if you're not attentive.

Covering All the Bases

When we speak about selling at the upper level of the Buy-Sell Hierarchy, we're emphasizing the customer's perception of your contribution. There's another sense of "upper level," however, that relates to the management hierarchy of the Large Account. In "ideal" organizational selling, these two senses reinforce each other. The best Large Account managers we know consistently present solutions to upper-level concerns, and they do so at the upper levels of the account's management.

This is no more than common sense. In any business, organizational and business issues are the natural bailiwick of senior management. In addition, people at that level are the only ones who can realistically commit their companies to long-term partnerships, and they're the only ones, in many cases, who can release funds. Good account management thus requires that you bring your upper-level solutions to their attention.

In recommending this, we're not saying that you should "sell at the top" and hope your senior contacts will impose your solutions on their "underlings." We don't advise anyone to ignore either lower-level issues or people who work at "lower" levels of an account's organization. Moving up the Buy-Sell Hierarchy is cumulative, not exclusive. Even if your principal contact is the CEO, and even if he sees you as a brilliant analyst of his firm's situation, you've still got to deliver the basic goods: the circuitry, the software, or whatever it is that you sell them. And you've got to check regularly how you're perceived by *everyone* in the customer organization who might conceivably have an impact on your two companies' relationship. This means being sensitive to Level 2 concerns when you're speaking with people who care about product specs, and to Level 4 concerns when the discussion is about improving market share. And it means, whomever you're talking to, making sure that they understand the value you're delivering: You've got to "merchandise" your contributions up and down the organization.

To address everyone's concerns, you need a team approach. In positioning yourself with large organizations, you have to cover all the bases: that is, ensure that every potential decision maker in the buying organization is contacted by the most appropriate member of your organization. But the appropriate person to call on the CEO is unlikely to be the same person who should call on the engineering department or on the accounting whiz who's in bed with your competition. In Large Account management, we feel that, ideally, CEOs should call on CEOs, engineers on engineers, and so on. You don't have to meet this ideal. You *do* have to cover the account's concerns from the "low level" of basic product specs all the way up to the "top level" of organizational issues. For that, you need the cooperation of a team.

Where Are You on the Hierarchy?

How do you know where you are on the Buy-Sell Hierarchy? There's no simple answer. But we can give you a few guidelines. If you want to get a fix on how you're perceived by a Large Account, we recommend that you first ask yourself these questions:

1. Where are my main contacts on the account's corporate ladder? There's a correlation between level of hierarchy relationship and level of calling. Since business and organizational issues are the bailiwick of senior executives, developing Level 4 and Level 5 relationships typically entails calling at the

VP or director levels. If you're calling below that, it's unlikely that you're positioned higher than Level 3.

2. *What are you talking about?* You might be selling multimillion-dollar computers, but if you're talking mainly about product features or benefits, you could still be stuck at a Level 2 or even Level 1 relationship. Remember what we said about the limits of bells and whistles. If you're talking mainly about your product, you're not above Level 3.

3. *What are you sharing with the customer?* One of the best litmus tests for the validity of a relationship is how much of your strategy and plan you share with the customer. We'll emphasize this later in the book. Let's just say here that, in building a relationship, trust is paramount. If you have "plans" for the relationship that the Large Account hasn't bought into, you're probably not very high on the Buy-Sell Hierarchy.

Remember, too, that not all the key individuals in your Field of Play may perceive you to be at the same level of the hierarchy. Where each person perceives you to be will have an impact on what types of conversations you can have with that person—and on the complicated texture of multiple relationships that you have with their firm. It's important to keep all of those different relationships in mind, and not make the mistake of "averaging." If Smith sees your company as a Level 1 supplier and Johnson sees you as a Level 5, this doesn't mean that on average you're a Level 3. As one of our more colorful sales consultants puts it, "If your head's in a block of ice and your feet are on fire, that doesn't average out to a comfortable body temperature."

The Buy-Sell Hierarchy: PreComm and Datavoc

With these questions providing a baseline, we recommend that you assess your position with your Field of Play by asking yourself—and writing down the answers to—three additional questions:

- Question 1: Where is our organization perceived *now* on the Buy-Sell Hierarchy?
- Question 2: Where was our organization perceived *last year*?
- Question 3: Where do we want to be perceived *three years* from now?

We'll use PreComm as an example here, and suggest the kinds of assessment that might be made by account manager Pat Murphy, in consultation with his account team members.

Question 1: Where is our organization perceived now on the Buy-Sell Hierarchy? For Murphy, PreComm is seen by Datavoc as being at Level 2. They provide "good" products—beyond the merely acceptable—but have not established a good enough relationship with Datavoc people (especially the procurement people) to say confidently that they value PreComm beyond the products themselves. "The proof of this," he says, "is that in the past Datavoc accepted our designs and then looked to see if our competitors could do the same, only cheaper. That's why we killed our design agreement with them. Obviously even the procurement people appreciate the excellence of our components, but that's not been enough so far to get over the push toward commodity. But it's way better than it was a year ago."

Question 2: Where was our organization perceived last year? Everybody on Pat's team agrees that the answer to this is "lower." At that time, shortly after PreComm withdrew its design arrangement, the tension between Datavoc procurement and engineering people was aggravated by mutual resentment between Datavoc and PreComm people. PreComm was still perceived as providing acceptable products in terms of design—Datavoc engineers were adamant about that—but the Design Innovation glitch had clearly damaged relations. "We weren't exactly at the commodity level," says Pat, "because their engineers were on our side. But their procurement folks were really focused on lowering unit cost. They didn't seem to care about lifetime cost of the components, and our unit cost, admittedly, was higher. So I'd say we were about on the threshold of Level 2."

Team member Robert Glock, PreComm's VP for Europe, doubts that their perceived position was even that good. "They were playing us," he reminds the account team with some bitterness. "That's why we killed the agreement. They weren't even vaguely interested in a Win-Win arrangement. As far as I'm concerned, we were at Level 1—and their numbers crunchers were intent on keeping us there." The team discusses Glock's observation and concludes that, realistically speaking, one year ago PreComm was probably "struggling to bridge the gap between Level 1 and Level 2."

Question 3: Where do we want to be perceived three years from now? Nearly everyone is tempted to answer this question by saying "Level 4 or Level 5." Murphy believes that's not realistic. He knows that developing corporate relationships takes time, and while his company might be ready to address Datavoc's business or organizational issues, it will take time to change their perceptions. So, focusing on PreComm's expertise in communications engineering and design, he suggests that his team aim for a Level 3, "service and support" relationship. "If we can reintroduce Design Innovation as a paid service," he reasons, "we can work with Datavoc engineers directly, rather than just meeting their specs, and overall should be able to reduce their R&D cost. This will also allow us to introduce newly designed wireless controllers and VoIP [Voice over Internet Protocols], which will significantly help them improve the flexibility and reliability of their systems, and give them a new platform for their telephony."

The account team agrees that, at the very least, this strategy should get PreComm perceived as a service and support partner. Cautiously optimistic, engineer David Olsen goes a little further. "If we succeed in cutting Datavoc's costs and help them capture an emerging market," he points out, "we may even be seen as impacting Chaucer's branding mandate, and that could get us seen as a Level 4 business contributor."

You can see from this example that accurately assessing your current and potential position on the Buy-Sell Hierarchy takes not only meticulous research but a good dose of realism. Keeping those requirements in mind, you should now be able to perform a similar position assessment on your own Field of Play. When you've done that, you'll be ready to move on to the next step in Situation Appraisal: gathering essential account and market knowledge.

CHAPTER 5

Preparing the Ground

"Knowledge is power."

—Francis Bacon

GOOD ACCOUNT STRATEGIES REQUIRE THE EFFECTIVE MANAGEMENT OF the right information. The better the information, the better the strategy. Therefore, once you've selected your first Field of Play and determined where you stand on the Buy-Sell Hierarchy, you need to spend some time gathering data. If relationship management can be likened to a farming operation, this step would be equivalent to preparing the ground. Unprepared ground, as any farmer knows, yields only weeds.

We realize that when you hear the phrase "gathering data," your eyes may glaze over. Maybe you've done your share of annual account plans that weigh half as much as the Manhattan phone book, and maybe you feel that gathering data is just another form of administrative busywork that keeps you from selling. Such common reservations are understandable, but they're misplaced.

At Miller Heiman we recognize the uselessness of much so-called account data, and therefore of most planning sessions. That's why, in this chapter, we give you detailed guidelines for getting the kind of information your team can actually use—that you can transform into leveragable knowledge about your Field of Play. We acknowledge that gathering such information will take time, and it will take coordinated effort from all your team members. But we strongly urge you not to neglect this step. It's the spadework you have to do to ensure results.

You've probably heard the acronym GIGO, which stands for "garbage in, garbage out." In computer circles, this means that a program can only be as effective as the input it is given. The same principle applies to Large Account management. The questions we'll be advising you to ask yourselves in this chapter are designed to elicit the richest and most reliable information available to you at this point. You'll use that information as input throughout the rest of the Situation Appraisal section.

Where to Look

Where do you find reliable information about a Large Account? Here's where we advise you to look:

1. Your own history with the Field of Play. This includes both past and "future" data. You want to know what you've sold them in the past two or three years, broken down preferably by product line and revenue, and what you're reasonably forecasted to sell them in the immediate future. Later in the book we'll present a reality test method for such forecasts; now you just want to have on hand your best current estimate of future business.

2. The account's reports. This means, minimally, its latest annual report. It could also include annual reports from the past two or three years, recent quarterly reports, promotional brochures, and product and service literature. These will provide you with this customer's view of its own position—something you must understand when setting strategies. If your targeted Field of Play is a corporate division or part of a private firm, the financial data may not be easy to come by. But even corporate business units and private firms issue advertising, promotional, and informational literature that can give you a handle on how they see themselves. The more you have, the clearer the picture.

3. *Investment opinions.* If you're dealing with a public company, assessments of its stock's viability can provide a useful health check. Such opinions may come from television commentators, from newspaper reports, and from investment firms' own published literature.

4. *The Internet.* With the instant research capabilities provided by the Internet, company information that a decade ago might have taken you hours to pull together from print sources can be on your team's laptop screens in ten minutes. Take advantage of that technology. For financials, for an organization chart (or the data needed to develop one), for articles in the business press, go to Google or Hoover's and the Large Account's own web page. That's the quickest and most up-to-date method available today for getting fine-grained information about a potential business partner.

5. *People in the Large Account.* In setting a strategy for your Field of Play, your team will be dealing directly with individuals we call Strategic Players. Ask them to clarify your understanding of their business. As you'll see, this is a technique that we'll be recommending throughout the LAMP process. It's especially valuable at the outset. Add to your knowledge of the account, and get a fix on where they think they are, by asking the people you're selling to directly, "What are your most pressing trends and issues?"

You may not know anyone in the Large Account who can give you this kind of information, or there may be no one you feel comfortable enough to ask for it. If that's the case, this is the time to start developing such a contact. We'll be speaking later about Strategic Coaches as critical resources. As a preliminary step in developing a Strategic Coach, try to identify at least one person in the customer's organization who (a) has broad knowledge of how the company operates and (b) has a personal interest in doing business with your firm. Information obtained from such a person can be an invaluable check on other information.

In addition to seeking out such allies, you should also contact account people with whom you *don't* feel comfortable. This is important as a reality check, and also as a way of bringing to the surface information that you need to hear but might not want to. Although backing away from unpleasant information is common and understandable, it's never smart, because it shortchanges you right at the outset, and frequently short-circuits your strategy.

Two further comments before we begin the data-gathering process. First, in LAMP analysis, whenever you discuss your Field of Play, you should do so from the *account's point of view*. Sometimes we call this "thinking with the customer's mind." It's seldom easy, and it often strikes people who sell for a living as unnatural. In fact, it's anything but that. From a purely practical, dollars-and-cents standpoint, you'd *better* see things as the people in your Large Accounts do, because the decisive factor in any business relationship is the customers' *receptivity* to what you're offering. That receptivity is inevitably a function of the way *their* companies, not yours, see the world.

Second, Situation Appraisal should always be done as a *team* endeavor. You should aim, wherever feasible, to come to a consensus understanding of the Large Account's situation. But recognize also that sometimes that won't happen. Team members will disagree about what's happening, or could happen, in an account. That's fine—in fact, it's valuable, because discrepant views shake up and test the analytic process. When disagreement occurs, write down the team members' differing interpretations. Have them explain why they feel the way they do. Discuss, compare, reassess. Good strategy setting is an ongoing process of refining your information. Divergent views often help to move that process forward.

Account Summary

We'll put these principles into operation now, in a three-part information-gathering exercise. In the first part, your team should develop a detailed summary of where you stand, right now, with the Field of Play. That summary should provide written answers to the following questions:

How are we positioned? List the names, titles, and locations of all people in the Large Account who might impact a decision about doing business with your company. Indicate those with whom someone on your team already has a relationship, and those that are still "uncovered bases"—noting any uncovered base as a potential trouble area, or Red Flag. Identify where each of these key players sits on the Large Account's organization chart; if you don't have such a chart, either get one from the Field of Play, or develop one. Identify the touch points in your organization for each of the Field of Play's key individuals. Consider finally whether there are additional areas in the Large Account—beyond your immediate Field of Play—where your company has contacts or might be interested in pursuing business opportunities.

What is our business history with the Field of Play? What products or services have they purchased from us in the past three years? Itemize these, along with the corresponding revenue figures, in a year-by-year chart. Then itemize the major sales opportunities with this Field of Play that you have lost to a competitor, and indicate as well as you can the most probable reason for those losses.

What opportunities are we working on now? Define specifically what business you're trying to do with the Field of Play this quarter and this year. Specify the products or services, the revenue involved, and the expected close dates. If there are any current problems or unresolved issues concerning these yet-to-be-closed sales, write them down, too—and note these as other Red Flag areas.

What are the purchase patterns? Do the Field of Play's purchases tie into a narrow band of your company's offerings, or do they show interest in a broader menu? Has revenue been increasing, decreasing, or staying flat? What market share does your company have for the products or services you offer? How strong is the pressure to commoditize, and how central is this to the Field of Play's corporate strategy?

What's the status of our relationship? Finally, write down a description of your current relationship with the Field of Play. In other words, where does your company stand, right now, on the Buy-Sell Hierarchy? Remember that your position on this hierarchy is determined not by you, but by the Field of Play. Has this position changed over the past year or two? If so, how? Come to a collective agreement about your position, and write it down.

The Account's View of Its Situation

Next your team should address questions about the Large Account's current business situation.

What significant changes is the account facing? In a dynamic environment, strategy must respond rapidly to changes that the Field of Play itself considers important. So have your team discuss the changes that the Field of Play would identify as happening now in each of the following areas:

- Their marketplace
- Their customer base
- Their product or service line(s)
- Their competitive position
- Their market strategies and tactics
- Their internal organization
- Trends and opportunities in their industry

For each of these areas, have the team decide which are the *three changes* that the Field of Play considers most significant. Write them down.

What's their revenue and profit picture? Write down what the account's sales and profits have been for the past three years.

Is there an upward or downward trend discernible in these figures, or has the company's performance been flat? Look at these figures not just in terms of the entire company's performance but in terms of your selected portion of the account. Most annual reports break down P&L figures at least to the division level; you want a financial snapshot of your Field of Play. Discuss also how key players in the Large Account *perceive* their company to be moving in terms of profitability. What are their expectations for growth, both long-term and short-term?

What are their KPIs? What are the Key Performance Indicators that the account uses to measure the strength of its business? Do you know how frequently these KPIs are updated? Who does the updating?

What's being launched? What new products or services is the Field of Play planning to launch in the next twelve months? Describe as well as you can their strategies and capabilities regarding these launches. If they have concerns or anticipate problems with these launches, what are they?

Do they have operational or business issues? Describe the key operational or business issues being faced by the Large Account's management team—especially those that may impact stability or growth. Are there plans in place, or being developed, to address these issues? Which individuals are responsible for carrying out these plans? Are any of these individuals involved in, or likely to become involved in, an internal reorganization? This last question invites you to consider the stability, or instability, of the organization. Is it centralizing, decentralizing, or in some other way changing its management structure? *Don't minimize internal changes.* They can critically impact how your Large Account makes both operational and purchasing decisions.

What's the competition? At Miller Heiman, we define the Large Account's competition as *any* alternative available to its customers—including an "internal build" or doing nothing. So ask yourselves: What other companies *or other options* does the Large Account see as competing with their solutions? In terms of corporate competitors, ask also: What's the competitors' market share as compared with the Large Account's? And what recent pressures are they feeling on the competitive front?

What other facts or trends are significant? Are there recent political or regulatory developments that may impact the Large Account's ability to do business? Is emerging technology having an effect in their market? Are they consolidating? Diversifying? Outsourcing? List and discuss here any development, internal or external, that individuals in the Field of Play may consider significant. And don't look just for those elements of the situation that relate to *your* business. Your Large Account isn't in business to serve you. Note and write down concerns that, for whatever reason, may matter to the individuals in your Field of Play.

The Account's View of Our Industry

Finally, being as realistic as you can, write a team description of how the Field of Play, and your various contacts in it, view *your* industry—and your place in it.

How do they see our industry generally? Start by defining what you believe to be their general attitude toward you and your competitors. Do they see working with your industry as essential to their success? As an acceptable part of doing business? Or as a necessary evil? What kind of contributions do they want, or have they come to expect, from doing business with you and other suppliers? What is their expectation of service and support? Admittedly, the answers to these questions may be subjective. But this doesn't mean that they're invalid, that you shouldn't trust your gut feelings about their perceptions— or that you shouldn't ask for confirmation about those perceptions from your contacts in the Large Account itself.

What's their purchasing practice? Do they always take low bid, or do they take value-added offerings into consideration? What kind of minimum specs do they hold you and your fellow suppliers accountable for? To what degree, and in what fashion, are they attempting to force your industry into commodity? Are they opening up or narrowing the vendor base? Note variation that might exist between different product or service areas, and between the account's divisions or business units. You want to isolate the criteria that are being used to decide between you and your competitors in your chosen Field of Play. Look, too, for recent significant changes in the account's purchasing patterns—and in your proportion of their business.

How are we doing, competitively speaking? Finally, ask how, in the Field of Play's view, your organization measures up against this general description. What strategic contribution do they see you as making to their success? How much market share are they giving you, versus what's going to your competition? How would key players in the Large Account compare your products, services, and support to those of your competitors for their business? How easy would they find it to replace what you provide them with offerings from another supplier? Discuss how you believe the Field of Play currently perceives you in terms of these important competitive categories:

- *Level of business relationship.* Where are you on the Buy-Sell Hierarchy?
- *Understanding the customer's business situation.* How much do you know—and share with them—about their driving issues?
- *Product fit to the customer's needs.* As a supplier, are you seen as marginal or as critical to their future plans?
- *Touch points in the customer's organization.* Are you connected through only one contact, or are multiple bases well covered?
- *The "enjoyability" factor.* Do they enjoy working with you, or see you as a headache?
- *Value of products and services.* Would they say the value you bring them is minimal, acceptable, or excellent?
- *Service and support.* Do they perceive your support as barely adequate, above average, or exceptional?

In making these assessments, you may find it useful to rate yourself—or rather determine how the Large Account would rate you—on a scale from 1 to 10. Use a 1 if the customer's view is extremely negative, and a 10 if it's the best it can possibly be. Once you've done that, you can then run through the same checklist and discuss how the Large Account would rate your competitor or competitors. Then compare the ratings. It may be helpful to write the assessments down in a double column, with your ratings on one side and your competitor's on another. This will give you a chart something like this:

Field of Play's View of	Our Company	Our Competition
Level of business relationship	9	7
Understanding of business situation	8	7
Product fit	5	9
Touch points in organization	8	7
Enjoyability factor	8	8
Value of products and services	5	4
Service and support	9	7
TOTAL	52	49

Resist the temptation to "keep score." In the example we've given here, comparing the competition's total of 49 with your company's total of 52 doesn't say anything as solid as "We're edging them out." The difference isn't that significant. Unless the difference between the two totals is large (say, 20 points), be wary of concluding from the numbers that either you or your competitor is better positioned.

Instead of drawing hasty conclusions from the totals, you should look at the individual *line items*. Then try to identify the *three* most important facts about how your team thinks the account would appraise the competitive situation. In our example, these might be the significant gap with regard to product fit (9 to 5), or the fact that the account sees little difference between you and your competition in terms of value (5 to 4). In addition, ask yourself the following questions, designed to qualify the numerical comparison:

- What are our competitor's chief *advantages*, as perceived by this customer?
- What does this customer need, now or in the future, that cannot be easily obtained from the competition?
- What would it take for the customer to buy from us what it now buys from the competition?
- In what areas of the customer's organization is such a change of purchasing policy likely to happen?
- In order for it to happen, must the policy be changed at a higher level of the organization than the one where we're currently positioned?

Appraisal As Reappraisal

The final question here relates, both organizationally and conceptually, to the Buy-Sell Hierarchy. It's appropriate to close this chapter by returning to the hierarchy, because nothing in an account's appraisal of a situation has more potential long-term impact than its view of your current business relationship.

We once found dramatic evidence of this fact in a LAMP workshop. Our client was a regional division of AT&T, and the division's targeted Field of Play was a major university. The AT&T people were offering a good product fit to the university's needs, yet they were having trouble expanding their penetration of this Large Account beyond a limited client commitment to long-distance service. "Somehow," one account team member told us, "they just don't seem to see how much *more* helpful we could be to them if they'd let us try."

Fortunately, the AT&T account team, following our advice, had invited the university's telecommunications chief to participate in the LAMP session. At one point during Situation Appraisal, the team leader turned to the university guest and articulated their frustration: "Just how do you see us, anyway?"

The frank answer surprised everybody but the university manager himself. "We've been buying from regional networks for fifty years," he said. "We see you as the new kid on the block."

An "objective" observer might say that seeing the largest telecommunications company in the world as a new player was inaccurate. But it made perfect sense to the university manager, and to the AT&T account team, it was a revelation. It made them recognize, in a way that no amount of market research could have made them recognize, that their hundred-year-old reputation meant next to nothing on this campus and that they would therefore have to take that into account in setting strategy.

In the words of the participant who'd asked the question, "When I heard that, it was a wake-up call. For the first time, I stopped thinking about how we saw the account and started thinking about how *they* saw the environment."

That's the basic reason you gather information in the first place.

CHAPTER 6

Strategic Players

"A company isn't a person. It's made up of persons. When you develop a business relationship, it's really the sum of those parts."

—Damon Jones,

Chief Operating Officer, Miller Heiman

ONCE YOUR TEAM HAS PREPARED THE GROUND FOR ITS STRATEGY BY gathering information about your Field of Play, it's time to start organizing it with regard to five critical elements: the individuals, or Strategic Players, you'll be dealing with; the Trends and Opportunities that are affecting the Field of Play; and the Strengths that your organization brings to the table and Vulnerabilities you have as you attempt to build your relationship with the Large Account. In the rest of this Situation Appraisal part of the book, we'll discuss these five elements. We begin with Strategic Players.

In managing a Large Account, you may deal with ten, twenty, or a hundred individuals who can, positively or negatively, affect your relationship. We advise you not to ignore *any* of these people, and in fact our Strategic Selling process is specifically designed to help salespeople identify all the decision makers in individual sales. In LAMP, we move beyond the individual sale to focus on the people who, consistently and predictably over time, are most likely to affect your relationship with the Large Account. These are the people we call

Strategic Players. They fall into three basic categories: Sponsors, Strategic Coaches, and Anti-Sponsors.

Sponsors: Authority, Influence, Support

The sponsor of a television program underwrites and endorses its activities. In LAMP analysis the people we call Sponsors perform a similar function for your account team. But not everybody who "likes" you, your products, or even your company is necessarily going to function as a Sponsor. To be identified as true Sponsors for your business relationship, individuals must fulfill three criteria:

Authority. First, they must exercise some degree of authority over that portion of the Large Account that you've chosen as your Field of Play. That is, they must be essential to making those decisions that will move your relationship forward. A Sponsor may be what we call an Economic Buyer: the person who gives the final yes or no to a sales proposal. But that doesn't have to be the case. Sometimes a Sponsor will be that person's boss—someone who doesn't get involved in individual sales decisions below a certain amount, but whose suggestion that his people "look into" something has the immediate effect of raising their awareness, of moving a potential relationship up on their radar screens. At whatever level you find Sponsors, though, it is their word, directly or indirectly, that makes things happen.

Influence. Secondly, Sponsors must be able to influence the *other* people who will be integral to your developing a relationship. In Strategic Selling, we caution clients against developing single-point contacts, that is, working relationships with only a single Strategic Player. The reason is that no solid transaction in a complex sale situation, and no solid relationship, can exist with only one point of contact or can move forward without multiple people buying into it. So if you have a contact who can personally vote your relationship up or down the Buy-Sell Hierarchy but that person has no support—or only grudging support—from other interested parties in the Large

Account, you don't really have a reliable Sponsor. A Sponsor must be able to get other people behind your presence in the account, so that it enjoys the broad-based support that a relationship requires. Sponsors don't have to have complete control over the decision-making process (in fact nobody has that kind of absolute control), but their voices must carry weight in the account. What they say must be able to have an impact on how you're perceived by the other people in the Field of Play.

We emphasize influence partly because, in seeking Sponsors, many account teams make the mistake of looking only at very high organizational levels—vice presidential or other senior executive levels—and then assuming that the senior person identified has influence in the account. That may or may not be the case. It's relatively safe to conclude that a VP in a Large Account has some degree of authority in decision making. But it doesn't necessarily follow that this person will be both able and willing to influence decisions about the relationship you're building. We know a VP of sales in a major telcom, for example, who has to refer every expense over $50,000 to the COO. The lesson is that you can't select Sponsors off an organization chart. You've got to dig into the account, to talk to the many people involved, to determine who has real, not just titular, influence in your Field of Play.

Support. This brings up the third point. A Sponsor must *want* to exercise his or her influence. He or she must, for whatever reason, be a strong supporter of your tenancy in the Large Account. Sponsors must see their own self-interest served by the development of a relationship between their firm and yours. Maybe they have been involved in a successful partnership with you in the past and increased their internal credibility as a result. Maybe they see the value that your company can bring as improving the productivity of their department. If a manufacturing manager, for example, was experiencing a quality control problem and he saw your firm as the ongoing source of improvements, then he could very likely become a Sponsor. By definition *Sponsors want you in there*—not just for a given project but over the long term.

Identifying or developing Sponsors is essential to LAMP success. It's possible, and desirable, to have more than one person serving in this role. But you cannot build a Large Account relationship that will last without at least one. If you don't have at least one person in the Large Account who fulfills each of the above three criteria, you should identify that fact immediately as a major Red Flag, and put your team's collective efforts together to remedy the situation. At the very least, you should list people in the Large Account that your team would consider reasonable candidates for this important position—and designate someone to set up a preliminary discussion with those people. Without at least one Sponsor, it's unlikely you'll be able to develop anything more than a Level 2 relationship with the account.

Strategic Coaches: Credibility, Support, Insight

A football coach gives advice and counsel to the players. He doesn't play himself but he helps the players on the field perform to their best. Coaches in a business relationship serve an analogous function. They provide reliable and usable information on how you can position yourself more effectively. In Strategic Selling, we speak of coaches for individual sales proposals. Strategic Coaches play a different, wider role; their impact on your work is account-wide. To have such an impact, they must meet three criteria:

Credibility. Strategic Coaches must have major influence, and often actual decision-making authority, in the Large Account sometimes even *beyond* your chosen Field of Play. Good Strategic Coaches must have high credibility with senior management and be respected at all levels of the company's hierarchy; without that credibility they could never get the coaching data that you need.

Support. Strategic Coaches are ready, willing, and able to actively support your efforts in the Large Account. Why isn't important. Whether the reasons are rational or emotional, political or professional, the Strategic Coach sees a personal

Win in promoting your tenancy in the Large Account. LAMP Strategic Coaches must be behind not just individual transactions or initiatives; they must give advice and guidance on the relationship as a whole and must want you in the account for the long term.

Insight. Third, Strategic Coaches are able to support your long-term tenancy because they can provide you the kind of insight that only insiders have. Strategic Coaches often hold upper-management positions in the Large Account, or are highly placed consultants with upper management's ear. So they know how the Large Account operates. They know at a high level what Trends are keeping the Strategic Players awake at night, what their strategies are, and what is driving the business. In addition, down to an operational level they know how it sets budgets and allocates resources and makes significant purchasing decisions—information that can be critical to you in setting a good LAMP strategy. To be identified as a Strategic Coach, a person must be able, and willing, to coach you not just on single sales efforts but on improving your perceived *position* in the Large Account. This goes back to the Buy-Sell Hierarchy that we discussed in Chapter 4. A Strategic Coach can confirm your position on that hierarchy, and can provide you with the information that will help you improve it.

There are obvious similarities between a Sponsor and a Strategic Coach, and it's not uncommon for one person to function in both capacities. A senior manager who can explain the workings of her organization and who wants a long-term relationship with your company might easily fill both sponsoring roles. But this doesn't mean that all Sponsors are (or can become) Strategic Coaches. A Strategic Coach understands the *entire account*, not just his or her immediate area of authority. The manufacturing manager with the quality control problem, for example, probably would not make a good Strategic Coach: His area of operations is too narrow. But the general manager of his division, or the vice president in charge of manufacturing— each of these people might be a suitable candidate.

As with Sponsors, the person you think is coaching you

must fulfill all three of these criteria, or you've got a Red Flag. If you don't have a Strategic Coach in place, you should make developing one—at least one—a top priority. In the effective management of account information, nothing is more useful than a top-level insider who knows how you're perceived across the Large Account organization.

Anti-Sponsors: Working for Your Failure

Like a Sponsor and a Strategic Coach, an Anti-Sponsor is credible to the buying organization. He or she has authority in the account and may exert influence on how the account and its key players are thinking. And that's the danger, because the Anti-Sponsor, by definition, wants you *out* or someone or something else in. Whatever else he or she may do in the account, as far as you're concerned the Anti-Sponsor's role is to *negate your efforts* to improve your position.

Sometimes the Anti-Sponsor's opposition is based on a difference in business philosophy. In the manufacturing firm that we've mentioned, there might be a financial vice president who seeks to block your involvement on the simple grounds that your company is not the lowest bidder. That person would be an obvious Anti-Sponsor. In other cases, Anti-Sponsors might see their self-interest being served by supporting your competition, they may be advocates of using internal resources, or they may be outside consultants who see your attempt to build a relationship with the Large Account as a threat to their authority. Jim Watkins, one of our sales consultants, once encountered serious opposition to his relationship building from a consultant working for another company. "We were competitors for the same budget," Jim says, "and he had a high degree of influence with key people in the account. So it made perfect sense to identify him as an Anti-Sponsor." What was true in this case is true in most cases: Whatever the reason, just as Strategic Coaches see a Win by having you in the account, Anti-Sponsors by definition see a Lose.

Internal politics is often a significant factor in creating Anti-

Sponsors—people who want you out over something as ostensibly "trivial" as turf rivalry. Countless relationships run into trouble because an Anti-Sponsor was categorically opposed to *everything* that a Strategic Coach or Sponsor wanted to accomplish. In fact, this is probably the most common scenario, and it explains why we call these people Anti-Sponsors; they are by definition opposed not necessarily to you, but to your Sponsor. In all of these scenarios, there's one constant: Anti-Sponsors oppose your tenancy in the Large Account.

Sponsors and Strategic Coaches are relatively easy to find, because usually they want to be found. Not so with Anti-Sponsors. Not everyone who is dead set against you, your company, or your Sponsor is going to come right out and tell you so. In fact, that's rare. Usually, you encounter situations like the one a software group met last year in attempting to build a relationship with a retail chain. The software account team was well perceived by two of the retailer's vice presidents and the head of its IT operations. So they initially couldn't understand why the resistance of one low-level player—an IT site manager—seemed so effective in blocking a deal they were working on. Closer investigation revealed that the IT manager was merely a messenger. The real opposition was coming from the retailer's COO—a man who had a personal relationship with the software firm's competition. This was a classic case of a hidden Anti-Sponsor.

When you find an Anti-Sponsor who's vocal about his opposition, you can count yourself fortunate, because someone who's blatantly opposed to your developing a relationship, who bluntly works against everything you want to do, is much easier to understand and to contend with than someone who looks like an ally but is undermining you behind your back. Many Anti-Sponsors, unfortunately, demonstrate Hamlet's observation that "one may smile and smile and be a villain." This is one more reason that developing multiple contacts in the Large Account is so important. Multiple perspectives provide you with a reality check when you're not sure what a given individual really thinks about your organization.

Almost without exception, having a Sponsor means you *also* have an Anti-Sponsor: The one generates the other. Therefore, developing an effective Large Account strategy always includes identifying these negative Strategic Players and exploring ways to "negate their negation." Anti-Sponsors can sometimes be converted to understanding that their self-interest does *not* run counter to yours and they can win from supporting you. After all, they're not actually villainous, just personally or politically disinclined to support you. Other times, they can be neutralized by the effective use of Sponsors and Strategic Coaches. The one thing they cannot be is ignored.

Additional Key Players

In every LAMP strategy, you ought to be able to identify at least one Sponsor and Strategic Coach, and be on the constant lookout for an Anti-Sponsor. But this in no way exhausts the list of people who may in some way—directly or indirectly—affect what you're trying to do with the Large Account. This is why we recommend that, even after you've identified the "big three," your team does some thinking about Additional Key Players. Even though such individuals may not exist in every relationship-building scenario, their presence is common, sometimes hidden—and potentially deadly to ignore. In identifying Additional Key Players, ask yourselves the following questions:

• Is there anyone else, either within the Large Account or outside it, who might impact the way this Field of Play makes decisions? Have we fully examined, for example, the potential input of outside contractors, consultants, or analysts?

• Who else might have a high degree of authority, credibility, or influence with the Strategic Players in this Field of Play? What about people who have been important in previous transactions, even though they may not seem to be central now? What about industry "gurus" or internal experts on technology, legal issues, or employee relations?

• Are there any critical touch points in the Field of Play that are not represented by our Sponsors, Strategic Coaches, or Anti-Sponsors?

• Do we have a gut feeling that a given individual is important, even though we're unable to define exactly how?

Brainstorming with your team on these questions, and coming up with honest, realistic answers, will help you expand your analysis beyond the "big three" categories, and may enable you to identify hidden players who could be helpful to your strategy.

Aligning Your Teams

Once you've identified all the Strategic Players in the Field of Play who will be relevant to setting an account strategy, you need to be sure that you align your team effectively with them. To ensure that, ask yourself these questions:

• Internally, have we established cross-functional links in our own organization?

• For each of the Strategic Players we've identified, have we linked that person to someone with an equivalent level of authority in our own organization?

• Have we ensured that, as the relationship moves forward, we have established links that will make the right resources available at the right time?

Alignment often works well where members of the two teams are linked through common interests as well as levels of authority—for example, finance people are aligned to finance people, legal to legal, technical to technical, VP to VP, and manager to manager. The role of the account manager is then to "orchestrate" this web of contacts to ensure that the various touch points in the account are activated as frequently as is necessary and that the contacts are made with a common purpose in line with the strategy for the account.

It also often helps to have a senior executive on your account team less as a touch point than as a "corporate unblocker" for those occasions when the account manager does not have either the authority or the political influence to make something happen that is in the interest of building the relationship. One company we know, for example, has all its regional VPs and country managers as sponsors on the account teams for its largest customers. This structure encourages country managers to support Large Account initiatives even if they may not be in their interest from a purely geographic standpoint.

Identifying Strategic Players at Datavoc

To bring this down to our real-world example, let's see how Pat Murphy and his PreComm team analyze the Strategic Players in the Datavoc account.

As Sponsors, Murphy's team identifies two Datavoc engineers. Pete Sanchez, one of Datavoc's senior engineering managers, is based in the United States and has, over the years, developed a good rapport with PreComm engineers. He participated in some of the early design meetings there and was convinced that PreComm's engineering design expertise was key to helping him bring new products through faster for Datavoc in the United States. He has made this widely known. In addition, Sanchez has a great deal of influence on Mark Duval, who is responsible for engineering design in Datavoc's European Manufacturing division.

The second Sponsor, U.K.-based Engineering Manager Alan Coates, believes—despite what his procurement people say—that the PreComm team can help him succeed both personally and in his role as the one responsible for the quality of Datavoc's systems. As one of the people who have the headache of translating Datavoc President Martin Chaucer's vision into reality, Coates is responsible for the engineering part of the manufacturing process and is under pressure to reduce manufacturing costs. He sees that even though PreComm's approach would not reduce the individual cost of components, it could simplify the number and range of components Datavoc currently has to use while at the same time increasing reliability. Coates therefore favors getting suppliers like PreComm to partner with Datavoc to remove cost from their supply chain.

As a Strategic Coach, the team identifies an outside communications consultant, Nick Constantinides. Nick has worked with PreComm before, showing another manufacturer how its VoIP concept could help bring it a competitive edge. He thinks that he can do the same with Datavoc. He is working with Datavoc's New Product Design team helping them bring new models and brands forward faster. He knows that if they can use VoIP, he can significantly impact their lead time competitive edge and simultaneously raise the profile of his consulting firm. He has discussed this possibility with President Chaucer and has relayed his interest in the idea to Murphy and his team.

As an Anti-Sponsor, Murphy's team identifies Dave Kaufman, the person to whom their contact in Datavoc procurement, Heather Rist, reports. Kaufman was Director of Administration a year ago, when PreComm team member Robert Glock decided to withdraw the design agreement it had with Datavoc—in Glock's view, Kaufman was the "chief numbers cruncher" who had made that decision necessary. The bad blood runs both ways. Kaufman has never forgiven Glock, or PreComm, for "abandoning" Datavoc, and so his major goal is to keep the components supplier out.

In thinking about Additional Key Players, Murphy's team realizes that they don't know anyone in the Datavoc organization outside of engineering and procurement—nobody, for example, in European management. That could be a real impediment to strategy going forward, and they identify it, appropriately, as a Red Flag area.

Finally, Pat's team considers how to link the PreComm and Datavoc players together most effectively—in other words, how to align with the Field of Play. They decide that, until they have identified other key players outside procurement or engineering, the team—with Pat and Sam leading—should focus on influencing Heather Rist, Mark Duval, and Alan Coates. On the basis of peer-to-peer contacts, Sam, with Alicia should he need her, should focus on influencing Dave Kaufman while Dave Olsen should provide the technical credibility to the relationship wherever needed. Because Robert Glock is still persona non grata in the account, the team decides for the moment that he should remain on the sidelines until Datavoc is ready to welcome him back.

CHAPTER 7

The Account's Trends and Opportunities

"People don't put money aside to deal with their vendors. They put money aside to deal with their opportunities."

—Sharon Williams, Sales Consultant, Miller Heiman

THE NEXT TWO ELEMENTS OF SITUATION APPRAISAL ARE THE BUSINESS Trends that are impacting your key account's environment and the Opportunities that are being driven by those Trends. It won't come as a surprise to anyone in business to say that Trends generate Opportunities. In making that observation, we're reflecting common business wisdom. Where we differ in discussing these two elements of strategy is in insisting that you look at them not from the perspective of your company, but from that of your account—and, more specifically, from that of your Field of Play. In LAMP, you help the account pursue *its* Opportunities, and only indirectly pursue your own. In many organizations, this would be taken as heresy. But it's central to LAMP analysis—and to maintaining the healthy relationships that LAMP supports.

With that proviso in mind, let's look at Trends.

Trends: Up, Down, and "Constant"

We define a Trend as any change in your Field of Play's market, its customer base, the behavior of those customers'

customers, or the business environment that is (a) significant to the account and (b) ongoing. Trends are fundamental patterns that impact the account *over time*. The time element is essential, and if you don't take it into consideration, your team may find itself identifying as a so-called Trend a mere transient shift in customer interest or fashion.

In the first Beatles film, *A Hard Day's Night*, for example, a pop star's agent nervously mutters "It might be a trend" after he hears a *single* negative comment on her performance. That's an example of navigation by paranoia—the kind of knee-jerk "situation appraisal" that leads to copy-cat and me-too "strategies." To avoid falling victim to this reactive brand of trend spotting, we advise you to look for Trends that have been developing for *at least a year or more*. Avoid the all-too-human propensity to focus on the one negative element among one hundred positive ones; those one hundred positives, not the one negative, are what constitute a Trend.

You've already encountered some examples of what we mean in Chapter 1. There, as we described the ways in which account management has changed over the past decade or so, we discussed the proliferation of information and communications technology (ICT), the rise in customer expectations based on that technology, the increasing importance of procurement specialists in pushing vendors into commodity status, the transformation of account managers into business managers, and the need to target account relationships with cross-functional teams. All of these are true Trends, and all of them have a direct, significant impact on the way account management must operate today. But other Trends that may be equally significant for your Large Accounts are not as obviously and directly tied in to relationship management. Consider the following ongoing patterns, for example:

- Increased foreign competition, both for markets and for jobs.
- Outsourcing (and offshoring) of noncore corporate activities.

- A greater public awareness of environmental issues.
- More litigation around product liability.
- Globalization of markets, supply chains, and manufacturing bases.
- The increase in virtual businesses and virtual offices.
- A decrease in customer loyalty and a rise in churn.
- Increased executive involvement in key account management.

To these widespread economic Trends, you can add examples of changes that are peculiar to an industry, a market, and even a specific company and customer base. Here again, to distinguish true Trends from market blips, the index you should look for is change over time. In the airline industry, for example, the attacks of September 11 had an immediate depressing effect on customers' willingness to fly. Yet that effect, while certainly significant—and certainly something that the airlines had to contend with—didn't last long enough to be considered a Trend. A more enduring impact on the national carriers—companies like American, United, British Airways, and Air France—was the success of no-frills competitors. Companies like Southwest, easyJet, Air Berlin, and Ryanair have succeeded in persuading customers to forgo the customary amenities (like in-flight meals) in exchange for rock-bottom prices and high-touch service. That was, and remains, a Trend that significantly impacts the major carriers' business.

Or consider a colleague of ours in the food concessions industry. Ten years ago, in dealing with institutional clients like universities and hospitals, she stressed the nutritional content of her products as almost a second-level factor: "When the benchmark was the Big Mac," she said, "college dining halls bought on price." Today, health consciousness is so high—with the institutions reacting to their end-use customers' demands—that it constitutes a major market Trend. A food concessions representative today can only ignore this Trend at her peril—and the same is true, of course, for the fast food chains; witness McDonald's and Burger King's introduction of salad choices.

As your team looks for Trends in your Field of Play's environment, you should pay particular attention to *direction*. A Trend might move up, down, or overseas, but it's unlikely it will ever be "constant." Few "flat-growth" profiles, for example, are truly flat—for the simple reason that the environment is not static. Say a customer has been a reliable revenue stream for the past five years—$250,000 in orders a year, every year. That may look like flat growth, but if inflation has been eating away at the value of that revenue, and if the market you're working in is expanding, then your "steady-state" customer isn't flat at all. In the environment you both inhabit, the real Trend of his or her business is down.

In spotting Trends a little pessimism is in order. Our advice is to look for negative Trends as fervently as you look for positive ones. If a global market, or the introduction of a competitive technology, or a surge in oil prices, seems like a threat rather than an Opportunity for your Field of Play's business, don't deny it. Threats can often be turned into Opportunities—but only if you see them for what they are. And if you work realistically with the Field of Play to address the potential downsides.

By working with the Field of Play, we mean just that. As your team develops its Situation Appraisal of the account, it will no doubt encounter areas of confusion, disagreement, or missing information. Our advice is to note these as Red Flag areas and go to the people who know the account best—your Strategic Players—to help you confirm or disconfirm what your team thinks. Because the very foundation of a LAMP strategy is a collaborative relationship, you should frequently check your assessments with the Field of Play itself. Nobody knows the Trends that are affecting them better than they do.

One final thing to remember about the importance of Trends. The Trend exists whether or not the Field of Play is aware of it and whether they choose to follow the Trend or try to resist it. However, very often Trends serve to trigger an event or condition that obligates the Field of Play to take quick action. Faced with a true Trend, your Strategic Players are likely to want to accomplish, fix, or avoid something now. Their willingness—and more often than not, their need—to do this, and do it quickly, presents them with what we call an Opportunity.

Opportunities: What's Driving *Their* Business?

To many companies, *any* opening in a market or an account is an "opportunity" not to be ignored. We see that as endearing optimism, but very poor strategy. We've encountered hundreds of situations where companies, eager to respond to every request for proposal, spread themselves so thin that, as Woody Guthrie might have put it, "even a politician could see through them." The fact is, you *lose* business by running to the door every time a so-called opportunity knocks. The strategic pursuit of Opportunities must by definition be selective.

That's an unusual perspective, but it's not radical. What is radical in our treatment of this third element of Situation Appraisal is our insistence that the Opportunities that your team should be identifying aren't Opportunities for your company, but for your Large Account. We define an Opportunity as the Large Account's reaction to a Trend or, in fact, as any issue or need that the Field of Play identifies as currently driving their business—for good or ill.

Like Trends, Opportunities can exist "out there," in the account's immediate environment or in the market at large, or they can be internal within the account. The fact that your marketing department has just put together a revolutionary new configuration for fiber optics transmission may (or may not) be a Strength of your company—we'll address the idea of Strengths in the next chapter. But it's not an Opportunity. When we speak about Opportunities, we mean the Opportunities that your Field of Play has to strengthen or expand its business with its customers.

LAMP client Paul Wichman, who is Vice President of Sales for Schwab Institutional, has an excellent rule of thumb to help his teams sort out mere market "tendencies" from true, business-impacting Trends. "It's easy to fall into boilerplate language when you're trying to locate Trends," he says. "So when I coach people about this, I ask them to locate which general patterns are affecting the way our *clients' clients* are making purchasing decisions. When they get that, they really start thinking as our clients do. And that's a critical shift in perspective toward what matters to the customer." This same good point comes through in the example we cited earlier about the British insurance company's working with its trade group Large Account; there, providing preferential rates was a response not just to the trade group directly, but to what its customers, the trade group members, had been calling for.

Or think about the food concessions example again. In this scenario, if our colleague were thinking about opportunities in the traditional sense, she would be trying to figure out ways to "place more product," that is, to increase the amount of concession business that her college accounts took from her rather than from her competitors: An opportunity in this sense might have been tied in to a special discount or a seasonal promotion. But when she starts considering Opportunities from the *customer's customer's* point of view, she sees that the college student's desire for healthier alternatives (a Trend) is driving the college's need to provide those alternatives (the college's Opportunity). And she starts to consider ways in which her company can enable the college to meet that business imperative. In the long run, she'll probably earn more of the college's business by adopting this strategy—but she can only accomplish this by "thinking with the customer's mind."

In looking for your Large Account's Opportunities, as in assessing Trends, your team must be willing to adopt a downstream strategy. Try to find Opportunities that, in your Field of Play's assessment, will have at least a one-year impact—and that, therefore, may take a year or so to accomplish. Don't get sidetracked at this point by writing down every step the Large Account will have to take to realize the Opportunity. We'll discuss those steps in the next part of the book, when we turn to Goals. Here, in Situation Appraisal, focus on the midterm doable.

Remember, too, that Opportunities come in negative as well as positive forms. They often describe something that the Large Account feels *needs to be fixed*. That might be something positive like opening a new market, but it also might be something negative, like avoiding a lawsuit or Chapter 11. If your account's "house" is on fire, it's not unreasonable to see putting out the fire as an Opportunity. So look for negative situations that may be driving urgency as well as positive ones that are promising growth or expansion.

If you're dealing with a public company, incidentally, one good place to look for Opportunities is in the Large Account's annual report—and specifically in the President's Letter or Chairman's Report. That high-level address to shareholders lays out what the company's senior management thinks is important as the firm goes forward, the issues that they see as driving the business, and the areas where they've decided to invest their resources. "Look in the third paragraph," counsels one of our friends wryly. "It's practically a step-by-step roadmap for 'Here's what we want to do.'"

It may be helpful, in identifying your Field of Play's Trends and their related Opportunities, to have your team consider answers to the following questions:

- Which changes in market dynamics (Trends) are having the most significant impact on your Field of Play's environment? Write down the three most significant of these Trends.
- Have these Trends been in existence for at least a couple of years?
- How is your Field of Play reacting to those Trends and what issues or business needs (Opportunities) are being driven, positively or negatively, by these Trends? Write down the three most significant of these Opportunities.
- If you help the Field of Play realize one or more of these Opportunities, what value will it bring them? What Trend or Trends will it help them address?

- Will realizing each of these Opportunities have at least a one-year impact?
- Are any of these Opportunities so good that they *must* be pursued? What would be the impact if the Field of Play were unable to meet the Opportunity?

As with Trends, even if you're sure about the answers to these questions, you should confirm your Situation Appraisal with the Field of Play. If you want them to see value in what you bring to them, you have to see the world through their eyes and solicit their input. If you're not comfortable doing that, what real value can you bring them?

Trends and Opportunities as Datavoc Sees Them

To return to our real-world example, here's how Pat Murphy and his PreComm account team might look at the Trends and Opportunities facing Datavoc. Remember that they've already defined the Field of Play not as all of Datavoc, but as that giant firm's European Manufacturing division. They've established a five-person team to grow a relationship with that Field of Play, and they've identified several Strategic Players within the account. When they turn to Trends and Opportunities—as seen from the Field of Play's perspective—here's what they find.

In discussing Trends, the team initially comes up with eight significant changes—above and beyond the changes that are impacting global markets generally, like the technology and outsourcing developments that we mentioned earlier.

- Trend 1: Increasing pressure from environmental lobbyists to reduce energy and resource use.
- Trend 2: Increasing legal pressure for health and safety protection of workers and consumers.
- Trend 3: Spiraling insurance costs due to product liability claims.
- Trend 4: Competitive pressures from low-cost Asian imports.

- Trend 5: Faster launches of new products by Datavoc's competitors.
- Trend 6: Reduced margins on European manufactured products.
- Trend 7: Increasing sophistication of inter-device communication.
- Trend 8: Consumer pressure for reducing telephony costs.

This list strikes Murphy and his team as concise and comprehensive, and they see that potential problems for Datavoc have emerged in three big areas: Trends 1, 2, and 8 basically reflect external, public pressures; Trends 3 and 6 reflect cost issues; and Trends 4 and 5 reflect competitive pressures. Trend 7 also results in competitive pressure because Datavoc's competitors will be working to develop products that take advantage of this. To get a clearer picture of which of these are really keeping Datavoc executives up at night, they ask Datavoc's communications consultant Nick Constantinides to give them some coaching.

"Everybody's alert to environmental and health issues," Nick says. "But at Datavoc, both the marketing and legal teams have got a reasonable handle on that. What most concerns President Martin Chaucer and his team is rising manufacturing costs, which are impacted negatively up front by European labor costs and downstream by liability suits. And of course competition in their global markets is always a high concern—especially given the recent Asian entrants, which can do everything cheaper."

After meeting with Constantinides, Murphy's team does some combining and hones the list down to the three most significant Trends that LAMP strategy recommends you identify. Their new list is:

- Trend 1: Spiraling insurance costs due to product liability claims.
- Trend 2: Competitive pressures from low-cost Asian imports and quick-to-market, more sophisticated products.

- Trend 3: Reduced margins on European manufactured products.

Working further with the information that their Strategic Coach has provided them, Murphy's team then looks at Opportunities. From the Field of Play's perspective, one Opportunity has already been identified—and spelled out, in fact, in the annual report. This is Martin Chaucer's mandated new cost reduction program, which he has tied directly to a Global Commodity Sourcing initiative. Other Opportunities, Murphy's team decides, should address Datavoc's other perceived concerns, global competition and slow launch time. They decide on the following three most significant Opportunities:

- Opportunity 1: Reduce production costs through Global Commodity Sourcing.
- Opportunity 2: Improve competitive position through quicker launch times of new and more sophisticated products.
- Opportunity 3: Reduce cost of product component failures and resulting liability.

You may have noticed—as Murphy's team certainly noticed—that in addition to accurately describing Datavoc's perceived needs, each of the three Opportunities identified here poses a problem to which PreComm might help to provide a solution. As a provider of highly reliable communications components incorporating VoIP, the U.S. firm may be well positioned to help this particular Large Account reduce its production costs, get to market quicker, and ensure greater product reliability.

This conjunction between the customer's Opportunity and PreComm's capability is not accidental. In fact it points to a litmus test that you should be applying all along the way in assessing Opportunities. Because LAMP is a Win-Win process, a true Opportunity is a mutual Opportunity. It's a problem for the account that you might help it solve. Therefore, as you investigate the Opportunities that your Field of Play needs to address, you should also be thinking about what you can bring to the table—what elements of product, service, or support expertise your company can bring to bear on the Field of Play's problem.

We call these elements strategic Strengths. We'll discuss them in the following chapter.

CHAPTER 8

Your Strengths and Vulnerabilities

*"The race may not always be to the swift or the victory
to the strong. But that's the way to bet."*

—Damon Runyon

YOU HELP YOUR LARGE ACCOUNT MEET ITS OPPORTUNITIES BY LEVERaging your strengths. That statement sounds logical enough, but it needs clarification, because in many if not most corporate environments, what people think of as their strengths aren't strengths at all. To get an idea of what we mean, pick up any annual report, any product brochure, any piece of marketing collateral. You'll find glowing descriptions of so-called strengths on every other page. Consider these typical examples:

- "We provide next-generation data-cleansing capabilities."
- "We operate profitable enterprises on four continents."
- "Our XVZ model has won prestigious awards for automotive design."
- "We are making significant investments in capital expansion."

These are impressive pronouncements, to be sure. And there's certainly nothing wrong, on the face of it, with advanced data-cleansing capabilities, global profitability, design awards, or capital expansion. But are these capabilities really strengths? The answer depends on how you define strengths.

In terms of LAMP strategy, that answer would have to be "Maybe" or "Sometimes" or "In certain cases." In and of themselves, these capabilities are merely that—capabilities—and it's not likely that any of them could be considered strengths in all situations. The only way to determine whether or not capabilities like these are strengths for you in your current situation is to find out what value your Large Account sees in them. In this chapter we'll show you how to determine that, by discussing a particular kind of capability called a strategic Strength.

Because we'll be discussing your organization's capabilities, it may seem that we're asking you to shift momentarily out of your customer's perspective, and start to look at things from your own point of view. That's only partly true. Yes, strategic Strengths are the solutions or capabilities that your organization offers the Large Account; to that extent they are determined by you. But their value—which is what counts—is determined by the customer. What this means is that their validity as Strengths is still something that begins and ends in the customer's mind. They're your capabilities or achievements. They only become your strategic Strengths when the Large Account says so.

To be considered a true strategic Strength, your organizational capability—what you're bringing to the table—must do three things. It must:

- Be seen as bringing value to the Large Account, *as its people define value.*
- Help the Field of Play execute against an Opportunity.
- Differentiate your company from the competition.

Defining Value

In Chapter 1 we mentioned that one of Silicon Valley's principal nemeses, in the early days of sales force automation software, was the user adoption problem, that is, the reluctance of established sales reps, some of them with dozens of years of experience, to take up computer-driven account management systems that their companies had mandated. This was a classic case of bells and whistles selling gone bad, and also of companies misreading their own alleged strengths. Excited by the capabilities of the product itself, the software providers assumed that those capabilities were also obvious strengths, and—being obvious—would sell themselves. But the target audience didn't see it that way—in fact, they saw the new technology as a make-work gimmick, making them *less* effective at selling than they had been before.

It was only after the software providers started to show sales forces how the new technology could improve their productivity, and therefore their income, that SFA and CRM products started to catch on. At that point, the customer had been shown a value that he or she could relate to on a personal basis. Before that happened, the so-called strength of the new systems—all that rich data-manipulating capacity—wasn't a strength, much less a strategic Strength, at all. In fact, because it alienated rather than attracting customers, this technological plus was a marketing minus. In terms of building relationships, it was a weakness.

This first criterion—that the value of a strategic Strength is determined by the customer—derives ultimately from one of the most venerable of Miller Heiman precepts: the idea first stated in *Conceptual Selling* that nobody buys a product in and of itself; they buy what they think the product will do for them. We mean "product" here very broadly. You can find Strengths in areas that go way beyond your products and services. Your company's core competencies, its brand, its reputation in the market, its delivery options—these and many other areas might be sources of strengths. But only if the customer perceives them as accomplishing something of value. In considering your strategic Strengths, that's where you start.

Matching to an Opportunity

There's a lot of talk these days about providing solutions—so much so that a colleague of ours with scant patience for jargon calls it "the single most overused word in contemporary business literature." He advises wryly, in fact, that you should not refer to paper clips as paper clips, but instead as a "hard copy linkage solution."

Humor aside, there's a valuable lesson embedded in the quip. We've moved from the age of great products to the age of "total solutions," and there's a danger, as we make that shift, that what we bring to the table, now called solutions, will be just as deadly in deflecting us from customer value as old-fashioned product specs were a few years ago. Again, there's nothing inherently wrong with providing your Large Account with a solution—whether you call it "tailored," "customized," "full-spectrum," or just plain "total." The danger is in assuming, because you've come up with a comprehensive package of products, services, and support, that your customer *must* see that package the same way you do.

The fact is that solutions don't have any more inherent value than products do. A U.S. company might, for example, be able to offer its customers 24/7 help line support anywhere in the world, and may advertise its global infrastructure as part of a "total solution." But suppose you're a customer based exclusively in Arizona, with no plans for expansion. How much are you likely to care that the company can answer the phone at 4:00 A.M. in Nigeria? In this scenario, the company's support capability might be a strategic Strength in Asia or Europe or Africa. In Arizona, it's not even a "nice to have" item.

Because solutions, like products, have no inherent value, we urge anyone doing LAMP strategy to match each supposed Strength to an account Opportunity. We described Opportunities in the previous chapter as issues or needs driving the Large Account's (not your) business. A true strategic Strength helps with the driving. It usually helps the customer fix or accomplish something that registers high on his radar screen. It may also serve to ameliorate a problem or eliminate a risk, in which case you'd be leveraging your Strength against a customer Red Flag. But whether you're helping to push the business forward or doing damage control, the principle is the same. A Strength is seen as valuable because it helps the account meet an Opportunity.

It's not unusual in good account relationships for a supplier and an account to build a solution together to address a joint Opportunity. The British insurer and its client, the trade group, did this when they collaborated on developing a preferential rate structure. But whether you get involved early or later, you must always test the validity of what you bring to the table against the account's own perception. Not doing this risks giving your customer the deadly impression—stated or implied—that you know better than they do what they need and should want. Acting on that false belief puts you roughly in the position of the intrepid Boy Scout who took an hour and a half to help an old lady cross a street—because she didn't want to go.

Differentiation

Our third criterion ensures that, in providing value to your customers, you don't neglect your own. Win-Win is at the heart of everything Miller Heiman stands for, so this criterion is in keeping with a long-standing philosophy. You want to build relationships, but you also want to win—and practically speaking, that means winning out against someone else. To help you do that, you should look for Strengths that are competitive differentiators, that provide you with measurable competitive advantage. A true strategic Strength is not just a value that the Field of Play sees your company can provide, but one that it sees you can provide better than the competition.

When Johnson Wax president Samuel Johnson was a product manager under his father, Sam Senior, he came up with an idea for an insecticide. The elder man asked him how it was different from what was already out there. The son had to admit that its features were shared by many other insecticides, and the admission made Sam Senior's point, that there was no competitive advantage to be gained in offering a product value that was already being offered by Johnson Wax competitors. So Sam Junior went back to the research lab until he came up with a product that *was* different—a water-based aerosol that didn't smell like an insecticide. Market testing showed that the new scent wasn't just an inherent benefit, but that the customers perceived a value in it, and the product soon led the field in domestic bug sprays. Plenty of other sprays worked just as well. But customers saw that only Raid gave them the *differentiated* value of a flowery smell.

Retail merchandising offers countless examples of this kind of differentiation, some that work better than others. But for all of those that work and bring their companies success, the three criteria above always apply. Whether it's a product feature, a service offering, a special level of support, an organizational capability, or something else, a strategic Strength is seen as delivering a competitively differentiated value that addresses a customer's Opportunity. If you don't have those three criteria met, you still may have something of great value to your organization—24/7 global support is an attractive proposition, after all—but you don't have a strategic Strength.

In *Conceptual Selling,* we argued that the *uniqueness* of the solutions you offer a customer typically impact his or her buying decision more profoundly than the objective features and benefits of a product or service. People perceive value in uniqueness. This is still true—especially as you work your way up a Buy-Sell Hierarchy. In LAMP, the perfect strategic Strength is something only you or your organization can offer. Next best is what you might call a "relatively strategic" Strength—one that, while not unique, is still perceived as closer to being "one of a kind" than anything your competition can deliver. The one "strength" that is *not* a strategic Strength (or a strength at all) is the me-too solution—the capability, no matter how attractive, that everyone shares. When everyone shares something, it becomes a commodity, and if that is all you have to offer then you will always remain at the bottom of the Buy-Sell Heirarchy.

A Reality Check: Vulnerabilities

The final Situation Appraisal element to identify before beginning to set a LAMP strategy is the one that many inexperienced "strategists" focus on first. Or, even worse, focus on exclusively. And such a zeroing in on the negative is extremely common. When we advise our clients to locate their strategic Strengths, the first thing many of them say is "What about weaknesses?"

Vulnerabilities are, literally speaking, places where you can be wounded. Yes, you need to identify weaknesses. But so many companies waste time trying to guard themselves against scratches that, on this score, we reverse the conventional wisdom. We say focus your efforts on playing from strategic Strengths, and focus your Strengths on addressing your Large Account's long-term Opportunities. When it comes to donning armor against your competition, concentrate on the *one or two* significant weaknesses that, if left unprotected, could cripple your strategy. Look for what the more classically minded might call an Achilles' heel in your relationship. Then take that Vulnerability seriously, and marshal whatever resources you need to offset or eliminate it.

Of course this isn't always easy, because "heels" can be hidden. In working to uncover and neutralize Vulnerabilities, therefore, we recommend that you keep three criteria in mind:

• A Vulnerability is *serious*. More than a Red Flag that you might be able to work around, a Vulnerability is something that, if left unattended to, can do significant damage to your strategic position with the Field of Play.

• A Vulnerability implies *missing value*. It usually entails a lack of knowledge, capabilities, resources, or something else that is critical to the relationship, and that the Field of Play sees as adding value.

• Even though a Vulnerability may be hidden, if key people in your Field of Play were aware of it, *they* would see it as a serious problem.

Given these criteria, it should be clear that a very wide array of deficiencies can be serious enough to be identified as Vulnerabilities. Those deficiencies can have to do with your products themselves, with attendant services or support systems, with timing, with individuals critical to the account, with shifts in market dynamics, or with any number of other factors that could threaten the relationship. Some of them, like serious product failures or impending bankruptcy, are obvious. Others become obvious because the Large Account points them out to you. When that happens, it's important to act decisively and quickly to correct what the Large Account has in effect told you is a relationship killer.

Here's an example with a happy ending from our own business. We have a relationship with a large accounting firm. Some years ago, we discovered that although its interest in our processes was very strong, its people were beginning to feel they couldn't implement them effectively unless we programmed our workshop exercises for computer. At the time—this was before laptops had become ubiquitous—we had no facilities for doing that, and we also realized that putting everything on disk would be a hefty investment. As the discussions proceeded, though, it became increasingly obvious that unless we found a way to deliver the extra capability that they saw as a value, we'd lose the account. So we identified the lack of computer capability as a Vulnerability, and did something about it, fast. By involving a software company in the programming, we were able to develop a three-way joint venture that eliminated the computing deficiency that would have killed us. It was an expensive proposition, but because it was the only way to maintain the relationship with the accounting firm, we decided it was worth the effort. And it did pay off—jointly. The digitization benefited us as well as the client.

In this example, early detection and corrective action were able to turn a Vulnerability into a value. But not every scenario works out this way, partly because most Vulnerabilities aren't this obvious.

For example, we once worked with a mid-sized consulting

firm whose biggest client was a Fortune 500 retailer. The consultants had entrusted this huge chunk of business to a single account manager—he had no team—and that person had basically one counterpart on the Large Account side. The B2B relationship had been profitable for so long, and the account manager had led in sales revenues for so many quarters, that the consulting firm didn't see this one-person-to-one-person arrangement as a liability—until the account manager abruptly left the company, taking the Large Account's business with him. That was a clear case of a Vulnerability ignored, and ignored until it was too late to correct.

One nuance to remember as you locate Vulnerabilities is that, as one of our sales consultants likes to put it, "They don't necessarily live at our house." That is, we usually think of a Vulnerability as something that's wrong with us—with our products, services, or support. Often, that's true—but not always. Vulnerabilities can exist anywhere, including within the Large Account itself, or in the wider environment of regulation, competition, and market dynamics. If you're in the mortgage industry, for example, a rising Trend in interest rates might easily affect your business as a Vulnerability. So, rather than thinking of a Vulnerability as something that's wrong with any individual party, think of it as a threat to the relationship that you're trying to build. Anything that could impede your progress with your Large Account, no matter where it "lives," should be identified by your team as a Vulnerability. Your team should come to an agreement about which one or two threats are most serious, and you should include plans for overcoming them in your Large Account strategy.

In urging you to focus on no more than two Vulnerabilities, we don't mean to deny that other problems may exist. Overcoming Red Flags, from the minor to the major, is an ongoing part of all LAMP strategy. In addition, in doing a Situation Appraisal, your team may very well identify more than two serious threats to the relationship. But concentrating on eliminating all of these threats at once is seldom effective, mainly because it distracts you from leveraging your strategic Strengths. So, if you uncover three or four problems that your team thinks of as true Vulnerabilities, we advise you to prioritize. List all the threats. Rank them in terms of their seriousness and urgency. Then decide which one or two *must* be tackled now. Those one or two, by definition, are your real Vulnerabilities.

It's true that you may have to deal with additional threats down the line—and that, if left unattended over time, even minor threats can turn into Vulnerabilities. But since you can't do everything at once, and since you have to start somewhere, we say that you should start with the biggest threats, and stay open to revising your assessment as the strategy evolves. If your car has threadbare tires, no horn, and failing brakes, you know you've got three serious problems—but only one that is likely to kill you today. So you put the tires and the horn on an urgent to-do list, and you fix the brakes now. That's a reasonable rule of thumb for prioritizing Vulnerabilities.

PreComm's Assessment

Here's how Pat Murphy's team assesses the Strengths and Vulnerabilities of their developing relationship with the European Manufacturing division of their key account Datavoc. They begin by remembering that a truly strategic Strength must (a) be seen as bringing value to the Field of Play, (b) match up to an Opportunity that this Field of Play wants to address, and (c) differentiate PreComm from their competitors. Then they identify the following seven potential Strengths:

- Item 1: "We have a long, profitable history with this division."
- Item 2: "We're one of only two global players in this market."
- Item 3: "We have enough reach to be able to manufacture the components they want in the least costly regions of the globe."
- Item 4: "Their engineers get along great with our engineers."

- Item 5: "Our design capability is second to none."
- Item 6: "We deliver on time, every time."
- Item 7: "We understand communications technology better than they do."

As the team discusses this list, Murphy's manager Sam Jones notes that, even though the historical relationship has been positive, it's fallen on some hard times lately, so that the history itself may not be a strategic Strength. "It's also old value," points out Alicia Carvounis. "We want something that they will see as bringing them added value now, and last year's shipments won't do that." The team agrees, and crosses Item 1 off the list. They also drop Item 4, for much the same reason. Murphy notes that, like Item 1, a good engineer-to-engineer relationship doesn't in and of itself bring any value; it's also too abstract to map to a specific Opportunity. Finally, the team notes that Items 2 and 3 are related, as are Items 5 and 7. Some combination leaves them with three Strengths that seem to pass the three criteria test:

- Strength 1: "As one of only two global players in this market, we have the reach to be able to source manufacture of the components they want in the least costly regions."
- Strength 2: "Our design capability and understanding of communications technology are second to none."
- Strength 3: "Our delivery is highly reliable."

Pat Murphy, acting as scribe, writes down the team's justification for these choices. Strength 1, they agree, can be seen as bringing value to Datavoc by supporting the cost reduction mandate of their president, Martin Chaucer. And, because only one other supplier can compete with PreComm in terms of global manufacturing sourcing, this Strength provides a fairly high, though not unique, level of differentiation. Strengths 2 and 3, design capability and reliability, can be seen by Datavoc as giving them an array of added value contributions: PreComm's design expertise has delivered measurable results for other manufacturers in terms of more reliable products and reduced product component failure—all action items on Chaucer's agenda. Strength 3, reliability, also has the potential for positively impacting one of the Field of Play's major concerns, its difficulty in matching its competitor's rapid launch schedules.

Turning to Vulnerabilities, the team realizes ironically that, from Datavoc's point of view, PreComm's track record with other manufacturers might actually be seen not as a plus, but as a Vulnerability. In fact, the VoIP team has had some of its greatest successes with one of Datavoc's major competitors— so the added value of design capability could turn out to be seen by Datavoc as a mixed blessing.

A second potential Vulnerability, the team realizes, is that their Regional VP, Robert Glock, is persona non grata at Datavoc, at least in the eyes of one Strategic Player, procurement head (and already identified Anti-Sponsor) Dave Kaufman. Kaufman, you'll recall, had been infuriated by Glock's decision to suspend the old design agreement, and it's not yet clear whether, with or without Glock on the Datavoc account team, he will be open to any relationship building with PreComm. The team knows that good LAMP analysis usually focuses on the single most important Vulnerability. But pragmatically speaking, this second one seems too dangerous to ignore, so they write it down too.

CHAPTER 9

Situation Appraisal Summary

"Reviewing the situation . . ."
—Tevye in *Fiddler on the Roof*

IN OUR LAMP CORPORATE SESSIONS, WE END THE SITUATION APPRAISAL segment by having participants summarize everything they've found so far into a single-page document. We recommend that your team do that also, following the review and guiding questions that we provide in this chapter. As a model for comparison, you'll find PreComm's filled-in summary on page 117.

Strategic Players

Out of the many people you deal with in your targeted Large Account, identify those who are most important in your Field of Play. Look for the three types of Strategic Player we've defined: Sponsors, Strategic Coaches, and Anti-Sponsors. And be sure to write down as well the names of any Additional Key Players that your team believes may have influence in this Field of Play.

A few guidelines. First, if you don't have a Sponsor, consider which of the people you've identified might be turned into one. Who is most receptive to your presence at this time? Could that same person, or someone else, become a Strategic Coach?

Second, don't be fooled into believing that you don't have an Anti-Sponsor in this account. The chances are virtually nil that someone in the account organization isn't antagonistic to, suspicious of, or in some other way resistant to your influence or presence in the account. Missing information imperils strategy, so, if you can't identify even one Anti-Sponsor at this point, mark that up as a danger sign. Go to the people in the Large Account who are most receptive and ask, "Who wants us out?"

Third, don't settle for identifying fewer than three or four players who can in some manner (positive or negative) affect your strategy. The goal is to identify, out of all the people your people are talking to, the ones who are key to your relationship with the account. If these critical individuals don't jump out at you now, you've got to find or develop them. The most tenuous position we know is to base a strategy on a single Strategic Player. If that person proves unreliable, is transferred, or dies, then your "strategy" immediately becomes a house of cards.

Trends

Now, out of the Trends you've surfaced, identify those that are most significant to the Large Account. Pick *three* and write them down. Recall that Trends can exist in the customer's customers, in its industry, or in the market at large. When you've selected them, check their significance by asking:

• Is this an enduring Trend? Has it been developing for at least a year, and is it likely to continue, for at least another, in the same direction? Blips or dips on a time line don't count.

• Because strategy capitalizes on Strengths, can you tie in this Trend to one of your strategic Strengths? If you or your team is having trouble deciding which Trends are most significant, ask which ones you're best positioned to capitalize on. A "megatrend" *you* can't use is not significant.

• Similarly, because strategy focuses on Opportunities, can you link this Trend to one of your Large Account's best Opportunities? If not, identifying it as a Trend may be valid but irrelevant. Consider, too, that the key players in the Field of Play may not yet have decided how to react to the Trend, in which case you may be ahead of the curve and can help them define an appropriate reaction.

Opportunities

Now identify and list in the summary the three best Opportunities that now exist for your Field of Play. Your investigation may have surfaced more than three, but you can't tackle all of them at once. So start with the three best, and ask yourself:

• Does this Opportunity exist in the *account* rather than in our organization? Is it something that they want accomplished, fixed, or avoided?

• Will concentrating on this Opportunity bring the Field of Play good returns for at least a year or more? If not, is the expected return from a shorter time span *so* good that it justifies their pursuing this Opportunity at the expense of others?

• Are there Opportunities that the Large Account would just as soon (or rather) address than this one? If so, it's not one of the three best. The three best are the ones they've *got* to tackle.

Strengths

A sound strategy capitalizes on Strengths by focusing them on Opportunities. In the Situation Appraisal work you've been doing, you've uncovered numerous Strengths. Eventually every one of them may become part of a Large Account strategy. For your current strategy and your current Field of Play, however, you should identify the *three* greatest Strengths you can bring to bear on the Opportunities in this account.

In selecting these three major Strengths, remember that you're looking internally. By definition Strengths exist in your organization, your people, your product line, your capabilities. But remember that to be truly strategic, they also have to connect uniquely to the customer, in a way your competitors' Strengths cannot. Therefore, ask yourself:

- What's the *contribution* that this Strength would be seen as bringing to the Large Account's business? In other words, why should the *customer* care that we're uniquely strong here? What value would they see in this?
- What's the specific Opportunity that this Strength will help the Field of Play address?
- Can this Strength be offered *only* by us—or at least *better* by us than by anybody else?

Vulnerability

Now write down your single, most glaring Vulnerability. Like all businesses, you probably have more than one weakness. Your decision-making process is too slow, or you've overextended yourself in a test market, or there's a muddled liaison between your branch and divisional managers, or you don't have a clear Sponsor in the account. Any or all of these weaknesses could hurt you. We're asking you to select the *single* one that, if left untended, could do you in. If you feel that more than one could do you in, pick the one that would do the job quickest.

If you find that there's real disagreement on this point, either you haven't taken the "killer" definition seriously, and you're hunting for any weakness, however minor; or you really do have more than one soft spot where letting things go could imperil your position. If you *must* pay attention to two, by all means do so. But having more than two Achilles' heels becomes suspect.

In identifying major weaknesses, there's never a single "right" answer. There doesn't need to be. Because LAMP analysis is dynamic, eventually you'll get to address all your areas of vulnerability. Start now by making an informed guess at what hurts (or could hurt) the most.

Check and Revise

You've now listed thirteen separate items: three Strategic Players (at least), three Trends, three Opportunities, three Strengths, and one Vulnerability. Your Situation Appraisal Summary should now resemble the filled-in PreComm model we give on page 117. Next, spend a minute or so on each item, justifying your selections. On the summary form, write one-line or short-phrase explanations of each choice. "Its expansion into Brazil is a good Opportunity because it's an untapped multimillion-dollar market." "Rich Onoro is an Anti-Sponsor because he's married to our competitor's CEO." "We're vulnerable in pushing the Series 3 transformer because we're still in midrange with quality control testing." If you can't come up with a good, short justification for each choice, it may not be as significant as you think. Rethink as a team and revise where needed.

Remember, too, that the Situation Appraisal Summary that we recommend your team put together is the beginning, not the end, of Large Account strategy. It should give you a concise, reasonably detailed view of where you stand now with regard to your Field of Play. But it's a provisional document, representing your team's best thinking about the account today. Due to the dynamic nature of organizations and markets, the summary *can't* be complete. So don't worry if it's unclear in some particulars, or if pieces of the picture seem missing. In effective Large Account strategy, information gathering and revision never stop. You've just laid the foundation for an evolving relationship, by describing your Large Account reality in the present. Now you'll look toward the future, and start building.

PreComm
Situation Appraisal Summary

Field of Play
Datavoc's European Manufacturing division

Strategic Players

Sponsors:	Pete Sanchez, Alan Coates
Strategic Coach:	Nick Constantinides
Anti-Sponsor:	Dave Kaufman
Additional Key Players:	No contacts beyond engineering and procurement (Red Flag)

Trends
Spiraling insurance costs due to liability claims.
Competition from Asian imports and quick-to-market and more sophisticated products.
Reduced margins on European manufactured products.

Opportunities
Reduce production costs through Global Commodity Sourcing.
Improve product launch times and improve technology lead.
Reduce cost of component failures and resulting liability.

Strengths
Global reach enables us to source manufacture in least costly regions.
Our understanding of communications technology and our design capability are second to none.
We deliver on time every time.

Vulnerabilities
Our history of working successfully with their competition.
Dave Kaufmann's antipathy to Robert Glock.

PART III

Strategic Analysis

CHAPTER 10

Charter Statement

*"If you don't know where you're going,
you're going to end up somewhere else."*

—Damon Jones,
Chief Operating Officer, Miller Heiman

ONCE YOUR TEAM HAS COME TO A DETAILED, COLLECTIVE UNDERSTAND-ing of your current situation with the Large Account, you're ready to begin setting strategy to grow the relationship. The first step in that process—one that is often neglected or insufficiently analyzed—is to define in general terms *where you want to be* when the strategy is fully in place and delivering results. If everything develops the way you intend it to, what will the relationship look like three years out?

The looking ahead that is implicit in these questions is far from a common trait in most business thinking, tied as it so often is to quarterly reports. But both practical experience and academic research have shown that the ability to visualize and define a desirable future state is a critical differentiator between successful and unsuccessful people—and organizations. Psychologists who study performance, for example, have discovered that high-achieving individuals routinely practice two "prepping" habits: They form clear mental pictures of what they want to achieve, and they write down descriptions of those achieved states. Neurological researchers haven't yet determined why there's a correlation between these two habits and success—but there's a scientific consensus that it exists.

The American mathematician Norbert Wiener, whose work on feedback was the foundation of cybernetics, referred to the importance of looking ahead when he distinguished between "know how" and "know what." It was much easier, he said, to develop the former than the latter—yet without "know what," "know how" didn't count. To achieve anything of value, Wiener said, you had to keep the purpose of your activity in mind. Knowing how to run a machine, a marketing campaign, or a business enterprise was useful, to be sure. But all the technical or management expertise in the world was still of limited value if you were unclear about what you were running it *for*.

Legendary American football coach Vince Lombardi once echoed Wiener's insight. When asked to define the difference between a good coach and a bad coach, Lombardi said, "It's knowing what the end result looks like. The poor coaches don't have a clear picture of the end. Good coaches do."

In this chapter, we introduce a tool called the Charter Statement, which is designed to help your team get a clear picture of a desired future state, of *where you want to be* in terms of your two companies' relationship.

What a Charter Statement Is—And Isn't

Usually, when people talk about their companies getting to desirable end states, the term they use to describe those states is "goals." We're deliberately *not* using this term here, because in LAMP analysis the term Goal has a precise technical meaning that we'll discuss in the next chapter. Here we'll just say that Goals are the intermediate steps or components that you have to achieve as you work to fulfill your Charter. They're important, but they're not the "big-picture" view that is provided by the Charter.

A Charter Statement captures the essence of your Large Account strategy, and it is therefore, by definition, a high-level, corporate document. But it's also tied directly into concrete, relation-based accomplishments that your team wants to make happen in the Large Account—and specifically in your Field of Play. A Charter Statement should therefore be distinguished from four other "planning" documents with which it can easily be confused. A Charter Statement is *not*:

- a wish list of potential transactions or engagements,
- an action agenda for quarterly or annual objectives,
- a forecast of anticipated revenue, or
- a corporate "mission" statement defining the CEO's "vision."

There's nothing wrong with any of these documents—they may each serve a useful purpose—but they should not be confused with a Charter Statement.

Some nonbusiness analogies might help with the definition. If you're sailing through a storm, a Charter Statement would describe the safe haven that you're trying to reach. If you're struggling with your weight, it would describe how you'll feel when you're fit, healthy, and thirty pounds lighter. Or—to take the example of Europe's most famous charter— suppose you're a medieval English baron. The Great Charter, or Magna Carta, that you and your baronial "team" drafts in 1215 describes the new relationship you anticipate having with your monarch, King John, after he has seen the wisdom of acceding to your demands. In all of these cases, the charter defines where you want to get to, not the intermediate steps that will get you there.

Here's how it translates to the business world. In LAMP analysis, we say that a good Charter Statement answers four questions:

- What's the Field of Play?
- What value will we bring them?
- How will they gain this value?
- What will we gain in return?

What's the Field of Play? We've already discussed Field of Play in Chapter 2, and we made the point in the previous chapter that, as you do a Situation Appraisal, it's possible to discover that your Field of Play is narrower or wider than you had originally determined. We reiterate that point here as part of the general LAMP principle that strategy making is a dynamic process, in which constant checking and revision is essential. So, assuming that your team is now comfortable that they've accurately defined your Field of Play, let's look at the other elements of a good Charter Statement.

What value will we bring them? In other words, what's in it for the customer? Why would they want to improve your relationship with them or, for that matter, to do business with you at all? As in LAMP analysis generally, so in the drafting of a Charter Statement, you should always be asking what real, measurable *contribution* you can be making to the Large Account's business. Not your business. To effectively manage a Large Account, you've got to see contribution through the customer's eyes, and deliver value that enhances its bottom line. Thinking about value up front lays the groundwork for sustaining and growing the relationship.

For most businesspeople, this is neither natural nor easy. When you're providing what you believe to be a good product or service, it's natural to assess its value from the inside: *Our* modem runs at so many bauds, *we* provide the fastest delivery in the East, and so on. But, as Adam Smith pointed out over two centuries ago, a market system doesn't tolerate so-called natural value: A product's value is what you can get for it, and that is determined, almost exclusively, by *what customers think it can do for them.* That's why it's essential to reverse the "natural" order of vendor thinking and state value from the account's point of view.

How will they gain this value? The third element of a good Charter Statement spells out specifically how implementing your solution will enable the Field of Play to gain the value you're describing. Here's where your great products or services do come in. But they come in as demonstrable proof of value for the customer, not as evidence of their own inherent worth.

What will we gain in return? We hadn't forgotten about your company, or the fact that, to survive, you've got to make a profit. We place this payback element last because it's common for sales-oriented people to put it first, and to risk forgetting about the value for the customer. But it's perfectly reasonable to ask, "What's in it for us?" Like all Miller Heiman processes, LAMP is rooted in the Win-Win philosophy, so we insist that, once you've determined the value you'll be bringing the customer, you also ensure that you'll be getting something in return. Ben Vreeburg, Sales Director at Loders Croklaan, a leading producer of oils and fats for the food industry, has this in mind when he cautions against drafting Charters that are theoretical exercises. "You can get very enthusiastic about your value proposition," he says, "but you can't forget that at the end of the day you have to make money, too. In a good Charter Statement, there's value for you as well as for the customer."

Sharpening the Focus

To make sure that Charter Statements are defined effectively in terms of both phrasing and content, we provide our clients a template. It forces team members in effect to put first things first. It looks like this:

The _____ (Field of Play) will gain _____ (contribution or value)
through the implementation/use of _____ (solution)
that we provide. In return, we will gain _____ (value).

Even with this template, however, few LAMP teams draft a perfect Charter Statement right off the bat. Typically, the first draft is so vague that it's hard to tell, from the written statement, exactly what the team is intending to provide and to whom. Some of them read like the TV astrologer's promise to deliver the answer to a question no one has asked. One example from a LAMP session illustrates how such statements can be sharpened into usable documents. The team was five managers from an electronics company. Their first-draft Charter Statement read like this:

> We'll increase our wallet share with General Aviation by selling them electronics solutions that give them state-of-the-art testing capabilities.

That was a start, but not a very precise one. It certainly didn't reflect thinking from the account's point of view. And it failed to meet the criteria of a good Charter Statement on several counts. First, the emphasis was obviously on the electronics company's revenue (wallet share) rather than on mutual value. Second, the Field of Play was not well defined. General Aviation, it turned out, was in fact a six-division multinational—a corporate octopus that couldn't possibly be analyzed or strategized as a whole. Third, "electronics solutions" was only marginally more precise than the vaporous "total solutions."

This first draft of the statement also didn't spell out what specific problems were going to be addressed by the seller's solutions. Nor did it define the contribution or value that the electronics company was going to provide. "State-of-the-art testing capabilities" was, like "solutions," a green term. It could refer not only to electronics but to anything from plastics to personnel. It was even difficult to tell from this statement what specific business the account team was in.

Most importantly, the contribution was spelled out backward. It said what the seller found of value, *not* the value the firm could bring to the customer. This may seem like a merely verbal distinction. Our experience shows that it's not. A good Charter Statement phrases the contribution *as it's seen by the customer*. The version given here didn't tell us why General Aviation would even *want* state-of-the-art testing.

When we made these observations to the team, they went back to the drawing board. The second draft was a little sharper, the third even better, and by the fourth round and the fifteenth cup of coffee, they came up with this final Charter Statement:

> General Aviation's Aerospace Division will improve their quality control and thus maintain their competitive advantage by implementing the most accurate electronics testing equipment on the market, which we'll provide. In return, we'll move from Level 1 (commodity) to Level 2 (good product) on the Buy-Sell Hierarchy.

This final version of the Charter Statement defined which Field of Play within the Large Account was being targeted (the Aerospace Division), what was the bottom-line value for the customer (improved quality control and competitiveness), precisely how they'd achieve that value (accuracy of electronics testing), and finally what was in it for the electronics firm (moving up the Buy-Sell Hierarchy). It was a close fit to all four of the Charter Statement criteria.

Here's another good example, based on the PreComm team's attempt to secure a better position with its Field of Play, the European Manufacturing division of Datavoc. After hours of discussion among team members, here's the Charter Statement that Pat Murphy's team agree upon:

> Datavoc's European Manufacturing division will achieve a reduced time-to-market and enhanced customer reputation by using our reliable, cost-effective components and VoIP technology. In return we will gain the major share of their overall spend in our market.

Notice how the sequence of ideas, that is, the *phrasing*, not just the content, of this Charter Statement follows the template that we provided. It appropriately begins by highlighting the contribution that PreComm will bring to the Field of Play, then spells out the how, and finally clinches the Win-Win aspect of the statement by indicating what's in it for PreComm. Another textbook example of a Charter Statement.

Admittedly, it doesn't always work out this way. Sometimes, even after four drafts, you still seem no closer to perfection than you were before the first cup of coffee. There are two common reasons this happens. Either you lack essential information about the Large Account that will enable you to draft an effective Charter Statement, or the team members who are wrestling with the statement view the account or the Field of Play in different ways. The cure for the first scenario is obvious enough: Get more and better information from all the sources we discussed in Chapter 5. The second scenario, while no less common, isn't as obviously resolved.

We witnessed this second scenario at a LAMP workshop where the client was a huge insurance company. The targeted account was another huge company—a multidivision consumer products firm. Ten minutes into the Charter Statement portion of the workshop, it became obvious that the account team was at loggerheads. Half the team members worked in the pensions segment of this Large Account, while the other half specialized in claims and benefits. So it wasn't Company A targeting Company B; it was two separate segments of the insurer firm targeting two separate segments of the consumer products firm. Naturally there was confusion.

The confusion was dispelled quickly and intelligently by an account manager who said, "Why don't we split in two?" They did just that, forming two teams, each with its own responsibility and Field of Play. And out of it came *two* clear Charter Statements. In other situations where team members disagree, there will be different solutions. The point to remember is that, as LAMP strategy in general is a team endeavor, so is the definition of where, collectively, you want to go.

One warning. It's tempting, when you work in a group, to slip into one-upmanship and point scoring. Resist that temptation. In LAMP strategy, while there may be plenty of wrong answers, there are few scenarios with only one right answer. The goal is not to draft the one "correct" strategy, or even to achieve complete agreement. It's to work, consensus fashion, toward a common goal: a clearer understanding, and thus better management, of the account.

Some Clarifying Questions

Since you can't (and shouldn't try to) simply "fill in the template," we offer some guidelines for your team to keep in mind as they mine the Situation Appraisal for relevant information and work toward a collective agreement on a Charter Statement. These guidelines are elaborations of the four basic questions that define the document itself.

What's the Field of Play? To help you decide whether the piece of business you've identified as your Field of Play is a manageable chunk—and the right manageable chunk—we recommend that you ask yourself these questions:

• *Information.* Do we have enough information to set a strategy for this segment of the Large Account? How much do we currently understand about their internal organization? About the people responsible for approving changes in the relationship? About the account's problems, threats, and opportunities? About the industry of which it's a part? If you feel less than confident about your understanding of the account in any of these critical areas, gather more information before you proceed.

• *Responsibility.* In targeting this Field of Play, are we within our own area of responsibility, or are we infringing on somebody else's? Suppose your organization markets internationally. As part of a North American account team, you might not be well positioned to set strategy for the Pacific Rim market; the Asian operations sector would be positioned better. This doesn't mean a North American team should never seek to tap a Korean market, but it may mean that doing so effectively would require cooperation between the American and Asian sectors, to determine who should be responsible for which actions.

- *Team.* Are we sure that every member of the account team agrees about the value of this segment? No account strategy has a chance at success unless its drafters buy into its potential, and the only way to ensure that is for each member of the team to see a Win in the ongoing development of account business. A marketing manager might see the Large Account as an opportunity to carve out a lucrative niche; an operations officer might see potential boosts in profit. The nature of the Wins is not important. But everyone on your team, on some level, has got to see a personal plus in better business from this account.

- *Priority.* Does this portion of the Large Account have high priority in terms of our current position and future account development? We've urged you to target an account where something is "off." We *don't* mean the billion-dollar pie-in-the-sky customer where you barely have a foot in the door. You should be focusing on a piece of already good business that strategy can make better and more reliable.

- *Position.* Can we be positioned with a broader segment of the account? We've stressed not biting off more than you can chew. Don't bite off too little either. If you now sell to only one of the Geoplex Company's ten plants, is it feasible that you could reach all ten? If you sell to Boston, can you cover New England? Can you move from division to group, or from group to corporate? Think about where your Field of Play might be broadened over the next one to three years.

In using these questions, some teams discover, as our insurance company client discovered, that they have to split themselves into multiple teams, each one covering a smaller Field of Play. Others find they're so ignorant of the account situation that they need more research before they can even begin. And many teams discover that their original Field of Play is too wide. It's not the Aerospace Division after all; it's that division's circuit board subsidiary. Use the questions to discover your own uncertainties and, if necessary, adjust your definition of Field of Play.

What value will we bring them? Now consider seriously, from the *account's* point of view, what value your organization is planning to bring to their business. This is always the trickiest part of the Charter Statement, and the part that makes it or breaks it. Your goal is to perceive your contribution as the customer will perceive it; that's the only way you'll know it *is* a contribution. In fact, one guide to developing a good Charter Statement is to ask how the customer would write such a statement. If you asked the customer to produce a description of a great working relationship based on the value you provide, what would it look like?

To determine whether this account will benefit by working toward a new level of business with your company, ask:

• Does the actual *phrasing* of our contribution statement put the emphasis on the customer's perception? Here, for example, is a vendor-centered phrasing: "We'll sell them our System B12 so they'll save money on inventory costs." Here's the same contribution statement phrased from the account's point of view: "They'll save on inventory costs by using our System B12." The distinction is subtle but essential. Only the second version directly and immediately answers the question "What's in it for the account?"

• Does (or can) our contribution deliver *profit*-oriented results to this customer? Can it help the account increase its productivity, boost its sales, lower its costs, or serve its own customers more profitably? In other words, does the "value" you're adding really affect the account's bottom line? If you can't document that this is so, you may not be making as valid a contribution as you think you are.

• How would the Strategic Players in our Field of Play define the contribution that we're making to their business? If the value you're adding doesn't make sense to them—if they don't perceive and acknowledge it as value—then it may not be as valuable as your team thinks. If that's the case, rethink and revise as needed.

How will they gain this value? Now define specifically which of your company's products, services, or solutions will ensure that the Large Account realizes the contribution. We mean "realizes" in both senses: The account must *profit* from your contribution, and the Strategic Players must *recognize* this fact. Some questions to help your thinking:

• What parallel and measurable contributions have we made to similar accounts? Can these be used as reference accounts to demonstrate the anticipated benefits of your solution?

• Are we trying to place too many different products or services with this Large Account? Is the account's interest as diversified as your menu, or more focused? Would it make sense to narrow your scope and exploit more fully the areas in which you've been most successful?

• On the other hand, have we been too *narrow*, too conservative, in our dealings with this account? Are there signals from their side that it's ready to consider a broader selection of your products or services? If so, which other segments of the customer's company should you be looking to for business? Which other segment of *your* company should be involved in developing this business?

• Finally, have we looked down the road? Based on your company's recent history with this account, what new business opportunities might be developed with it in the next year? The next three? The next ten?

With these questions in mind, make appropriate revisions to your Charter Statement. Ideally, your Charter Statement should indicate not only what contribution you are making right now, but also, thinking one to three years out, what additional value you might provide under a stronger relationship.

What will we get in return? Finally, to ensure that the relationship you're seeking to develop will be mutually beneficial, define how your organization will profit if your strategy is successful. "Profit" may include anticipated revenue, but it doesn't need to be—indeed, usually shouldn't be—confined to that. Define what broad gains, in terms of position as well as income, you want to have accruing to your company. Then test these gains by asking:

- Are they *realistic?* Given everything you've found in the Situation Appraisal—including the Large Account's receptivity to your company and your ability to marshal resources to meet their needs—how likely is it that these gains can be realized in the next one to three years?
- Are they *fair?* That is, are they commensurate with the time and resources you're planning to devote to the account? If you're "paid" with these gains, will that be a reasonable return on your investment?
- How will we *measure* them? On the balance sheets? In terms of customer testimonials? In terms of new legal arrangements? If you're truly playing Win-Win, then in three years (or less) you should have concrete evidence that the relationship you've been building is helping both your organizations.

Some Final Tests

Finally, here are a few additional questions, designed to help you test your draft Charter Statement against reality. These questions are the acid tests. If your team can't answer them positively and enthusiastically, you might want to rethink your perception of the Field of Play, and to reconsider whether this Charter Statement really defines accurately where you want to go.

Would our Strategic Players understand this Charter Statement without a lot of explanation? If the statement isn't crystal clear to the people whose business it's designed to be helping, it won't matter how technically or conceptually ingenious it is. The Charter Statement should define, without jargon and without complex implementation scenarios, how you'd like your two companies to be working together. They've got to be able to "get it" without elaborate explanation.

If we took our name off the Charter Statement, would they recog-

nize us from what the statement says? A good Charter Statement defines the desired business relationship between you and the account. If people at the account wouldn't be able to "see" you in the Charter Statement—if they can't distinguish your company in this statement from statements that your competitors might draft—then either you're not clearly differentiated from other vendors or you haven't yet defined clearly enough the special value that you're bringing to the customer's business.

If we get to this desired state, will we attain our targeted position(s) on the Buy-Sell Hierarchy? Whatever your position is now—and remember that it may be different with different Strategic Players—and wherever your team wants to be three years from now, the Charter Statement should define your desired relationships both with those key individuals and—to the degree that this is possible—with the Field of Play as a whole. If your Charter Statement doesn't implicitly or explicitly describe a desirable hierarchy position, it probably needs some reworking or rephrasing.

Are we willing to share this Charter Statement with the Strategic Players? This is both the most unusual and the most critical of the four questions. It's unusual because few companies are so market-driven that they're ready to include their customers in strategy sessions. It's critical because, as literally hundreds of our clients have proven time and again, sharing where you want to go with the people you want to get there with is the single most reliable test, especially in the early stages of strategy, for whether the relationship you're interested in building has a chance of success. On this level at least, building a corporate relationship isn't all that different from building a personal relationship. Imagine a marriage in which the husband has a clear vision of where he wants the relationship to be in five years— but isn't willing to share that vision with his new wife. What are the chances that these two people are even going to be *together* in five years, much less at the "ideal state" that the husband has in mind?

Companies with the most effective account strategies have built the principle of sharing the Charter Statement into the organizational structure of strategy setting. For example, we've actually run workshops where, after drafting a Charter Statement, the account team will bring in Strategic Players from its Large Account to verify that their two companies are on the same page. After one of those workshops, we heard one Large Account representative say, with considerable surprise, "You know, this is the first time we've felt that you guys are actually interested in how we look at you." That was an invaluable step forward in the relationship.

At our client Schwab Institutional, to give a second example, the client base is segmented into multiple tiers, with the top tier, Premium Clients, under the direct account management authority of regional vice presidents. According to the company's Vice President of Sales, Paul Wichman, "Each regional VP might have responsibility for five to ten of these top-tier clients. That's important business for us, and we want to be sure that those clients know, at every step of the way, how important we consider them. In LAMP strategy, we accomplish that by requiring that the account managers sit down with those clients once a year and have them completely vet a Charter Statement. This isn't optional. It's one way we continue to make sure that we're serving these Premium Clients to the best of our ability."

A similar protocol is in place at Experian, the United Kingdom's leading credit reference agency. The company's Sales Director, Tony Leach, acknowledges that sharing the Charter Statement and other strategy information with customers doesn't come naturally. "It's often a matter of confidence," he explains. "If you're not really sure about how Strategic Players in an account see you, it feels risky to share your analysis with them directly. Especially risky to say, 'We think Bob Baxter is our Anti-Sponsor.' So people are often reluctant to do this directly, and they try to convince themselves that their picture of the account is private information. But that's actually far more risky than sharing it. You really need to sit down with your clients and get their feedback. Sharing the Charter Statement is an essential sanity check as you go forward."

Paul and Tony have it exactly right. As their companies and

so many other industry leaders have discovered, the quickest way to find out whether or not you're on the same page with your customers is to write out a Charter Statement—and then *show them that page*. Doing this periodically, as Paul's statement suggests, helps you keep track of your customers' constantly changing business needs. Like everything else in a good LAMP strategy, the Charter Statement should be viewed not as a graven-in-stone game plan, but as a dynamic tool, providing a solid estimate of where the relationship should be heading, but subject to frequent revision as conditions evolve.

CHAPTER 11

Goals

"O! that a man might know
The end of this day's business, ere it come."

—Brutus in *Julius Caesar*

WE'VE SAID THAT THE CHARTER STATEMENT DESCRIBES WHERE YOUR account team wants to go, the "destination" of your strategy. Some of our process experts use a sailing metaphor to clarify this point: The Charter, they say, is a description of the "port" you want to arrive at, once your strategic plans have been put into place.

Sailors don't approach ports in a straight line. Instead, to take advantage of varying winds, they tack back and forth in the direction of their destination, so that the typical approach path more nearly resembles a series of zigzagging steps than a straight shot from the middle of the ocean to a safe harbor. The same principle applies in LAMP strategy. To get safely into the harbor of your Charter Statement, you proceed in a series of necessary, incremental steps. Those steps don't zigzag—like any metaphor, this one isn't exact—but they do resemble a sailor's tacking motion in that it's the aggregate effect of those component motions that gets you home.

In LAMP, we call these steps Goals, and we think of them as incremental stages toward better points of value. In this chapter we'll explain how our definition of Goals differs from other, more widely used definitions, and we'll show how setting realistic, incremental Goals contributes to the realization of a Charter Statement—how, in effect, they actualize the Charter.

Why Traditional "Goals" Often Fail

In order to actualize a Charter, your Goals have to be realistic, and they have to be tied in precisely to your Large Account's perceptions. The "goals" that most organizations set for their people seldom succeed in fulfilling this dual requirement. In fact, most companies set corporate goals that are impossibly vague ("Increase our market share") while setting sales goals that are just as impossibly precise ("Boost fall quarter revenues by 7.5 percent"). This double confusion leads them, not infrequently, into a fool's paradise of wish fulfillment where true Goals are subordinated to computer-assisted "projections" that bear little or no relation to achievable results. In this fool's paradise, typical "goals" are unrealistic in three ways.

First, they're generated by *past* rather than current realities, so at best they can never be more than sophisticated guesses, or quarterly "projections."

Second, they're too *vendor-focused*. Most corporate goal setting forgets the cardinal rule that the *account* ultimately decides whether or not your goals are met—and that it decides on the basis of *its* needs, not yours.

Third, they're exclusively *quantitative*. Focused on cash flow charts and market projection specs, businesses attempt to operate by the numbers and to insist that all goals must be *measurable* on the balance sheets.

In this strategy-setting part of the LAMP process, you'll define Goals that avoid these three errors. You'll be able to do so because you'll be following a unique definition: In LAMP strategy, a Goal is a *qualitative* position that the Large Account endorses and validates.

Goals: The Qualitative Dimension

It's not that quantification and revenue aren't important. Of course they are—and we'll discuss just how important in a later chapter, when we consider the Win-Win aspects of meeting Revenue Targets. But revenue should never be considered paramount when you're defining Goals, because most Goals— as we define them in LAMP—cannot be counted as you count capital expenditures or licensing fees or personnel costs. We realize that, in an economy driven by the profit motive, this may sound heretical. But it's true. You can measure revenue, and payroll, and operating costs. But in the long-term management of Large Accounts, true Goals do not appear on the spreadsheets.

Part of the reason lies in that familiar phrase "long-term." Because LAMP defines Goals as desired relational positions, and because solid positioning never happens overnight, we say that the interim results you should be aiming for—the steps that will get you closer to your Charter—will typically take a year or more to achieve. If you're looking at an accomplishment that you expect to tie down in six weeks, it may indeed be critical to account success. But it's not what we define in LAMP as a Goal.

Another reason is that Goals are achieved only when your Large Account agrees they've been achieved—often because meeting your Goals is a signal that the people in the account have met *their* goals. In a sense, when you lay out your Goals, you're setting your sights on mind share—your Strategic Players' mental commitment to an ongoing relationship with your company. Just as the validity of your Charter Statement "contribution" and the level of your business relationship are ultimately defined by the Large Account itself, indirectly so are your Goals. In fact, a shorthand way of looking at your Goal is as a link between the Charter Statement and the Buy-Sell Hierarchy. Meeting a specific Goal should help to validate the contribution promise of your Charter Statement. Meeting multiple

Goals in sequence should help to improve your position in the relational hierarchy.

The Importance of Phrasing

To ensure that the element of mind share is not forgotten, we say that you should always *write down* your Goals in a specific, client-centered formula—one whose very sentence structure emphasizes how *clients* see *you*. This formula also forces account teams to devise Goals that have a good chance of addressing clients' Opportunities and leveraging the supplying company's own strategic Strengths. Here's the formula:

> Be _____ (seen, known, acknowledged, recognized)
> by _____ (Field of Play, Strategic Players)
> as the _____ (supplier, partner, consultant, expert)
> who helped achieve _____ (Opportunity)
> through _____ (Strength).

To see how this formula works out in practice, recall the Charter Statement that one of our clients drafted in its targeting of the Aerospace Division of General Aviation. In that statement, the account team promised to provide "the most accurate electronics testing equipment on the market," so that the customer could maintain its competitive advantage through improved quality control. Here's the first draft of a Goal that was supposed to deliver on that promise:

Goal:
To replace their current patchwork in-house quality control system with our more reliable, unified approach.

That was a start, but it sounded more like a sales objective than a Goal, because the team was looking through the wrong end of the telescope. With this phrasing, you could tell that accomplishing the Goal would be good for them, but not what it would do for the customer. When we asked the team to rephrase it from the customer's perspective, they came up with this second draft:

Goal:

To provide the client greater quality control reliability by replacing their patchwork in-house system with our unified systems approach.

That was better. Simply by rearranging the sentence, by substituting "replace" with "provide," and by introducing the critical word "reliability," the team put greater emphasis on the account. But the element of mind share was still foggy. So we underlined the importance of the customer's *perception* of reality. Because strategic position is always in the mind of the beholder, it's important to phrase your Goal statements so they emphasize the way you want *to be seen* by the Strategic Players in your Large Account. With that clarification—and the LAMP phrasing formula—in mind, the account team finally produced this copy:

Goal:

To be seen by the Aerospace Division as the supplier that brought them greater quality control reliability by upgrading their patchwork in-house system with a unified systems approach.

This version hit the mark. Even though the wording changes between the second and third drafts were admittedly minor, they accomplished a critical shift in perspective, moving the focus subtly away from the seller's contribution to the way the customer would *see* that contribution. The value-added "reliability" was important, to be sure. But the improved position that the team was eventually able to secure in this account didn't come from reliability in the abstract. It came from the customer's *perception* of this supplier as the provider of that business result. Notice, too, how this final phrasing identified clearly the customer Opportunity (more reliable QC) that was to be addressed, and the strategic Strength (unified systems approach) that would help address it.

Our insistence on this formula is not just semantics. We've worked with hundreds of Fortune 500 revenue leaders. Many of them accuse us of playing with words when we insist on the "Be seen as" phrasing—until they realize how this "merely semantic" device helps them see themselves as the account is seeing them. And what an impact it can make with the Large Account's key players when you share a Goals statement with them and demonstrate that you take their perspective seriously.

The PreComm Case

For further examples of Goals stated from the account's point of view, let's look at the ones that the PreComm team came up with to help actualize its Charter Statement. You'll recall that the Charter read like this:

Datavoc's European Manufacturing division will achieve a reduced time-to-market and enhanced consumer reputation by using our reliable, cost-effective components and VoIP technology. In return we will gain the major share of their overall spend in our market.

Here are the PreComm account team's suggested Goals, relating to the key Datavoc players that were identified in Chapter 6. We'll explain the material in the parentheses in a moment.

- Be seen by Alan Coates as the supplier on whom he could rely for components with good reliability and minimum Dead on Arrivals (Level 2).
- Be acknowledged by procurement as the vendor with the best performance in terms of flexibility and just-in-time delivery (Level 3).
- Be acknowledged by Heather Rist to Dave Kaufman as the supplier that offers best whole-life component costs versus unit base price (Level 2).
- Be seen by Dave Kaufman as having done enough to reverse the damage done by our negation of the design agreement (eliminate Vulnerability).
- Be recommended by Pete Sanchez to Mark Duval as the expert design partner for the next family of Datavoc's air-conditioning controller units (Level 3).
- Be seen by Datavoc's European Manufacturing board as the supplier who helped them consistently control costs (Level 3 or 4).

Notice several things about these sample Goals. First, although none of them gets down to measurable nuts and bolts, none of them is vague either. When we say that true Goals are qualitative, we don't mean they're wishy-washy or abstract. In the General Aviation example, the Goal hooked up specifically to quality control improvement. In the examples given here, there are also clearly defined business elements: "whole life component costs," "reliability," "expert design." Like the "contribution" section of a Charter Statement, Goals should define specific ends that relate to your business, the customer's business, and your relationship.

Second, the Goals describe not just how the PreComm team wants its company to be seen by Datavoc in general, but how they want to be perceived by specific Strategic Players in their Field of Play. It's not unreasonable to speak of two companies having a relationship, but for practical purposes that relationship will always play itself out in terms of individual activities and personal perceptions. That's why PreComm defines Goals that will help to build healthy relationships with key individuals. The aggregate of those relationships will in effect equal the corporate relationship. But you can't build that whole without the sum of the parts. That's why, ideally, each Goal should satisfy the personal or professional needs of one or more Strategic Players.

Third, see how the Goals, either implicitly or explicitly, define the way in which a PreComm Strength can impact a Datavoc Opportunity. In assessing their Strengths, the team saw that PreComm's global reach enabled them to (a) source component manufacture in the least costly regions, (b) provide unparalleled design capability, and (c) provide absolutely reliable delivery. They wanted to leverage those Strengths against three Datavoc Opportunities: (a) reduced production costs, (b) quicker launch times, and (c) reduced component failures. So, for example, in writing the first Goal above, they leveraged their reliability (Strength) to address engineer Coates's need for predictable component delivery (Opportunity). For the fifth, they leveraged their design skills (Strength) to address a next-generation product development (Opportunity). Similar match-ups of Strengths and Opportunities can be seen in the other Goals.

Fourth, you'll see that one of the Goals, rather than leveraging a Strength, attempts to offset a Vulnerability. We've said that you should always work from Strength. But when faced with a clear Vulnerability, as the PreComm team is here, it makes good sense to address that at the Goal-setting stage. In this case, offsetting the bad history between the two companies is definitely something that the team would want to consider, and making that a Goal is not inappropriate—especially since it is Dave Kaufman, the Anti-Sponsor, whose perception of PreComm the team is trying to improve.

Finally, notice that, for each Goal, the team has identified a level of the Buy-Sell Hierarchy (indicated in the parentheses) where achievement of this Goal would help to better position PreComm. There are multiple levels, each one corresponding to a specific Strategic Player's perception of the relationship. Again, this is appropriate, given the fact that, in building a relationship, you're necessarily dealing with individuals who comprise the Large Account and who have different perceptions of the relationship, and of where they would like you to be positioned on the hierarchy. In this context it's useful to remember that both Goals and the Charter Statement will very likely have to be written differently depending on where you are on the Buy-Sell Hierarchy.

Generating Goals

You can't realistically work toward achieving more than a few long-term Goals at a time. In LAMP sessions, we advise our clients to limit themselves at first to the *three* most significant Goals that they want to accomplish. Since LAMP depends so much on interaction, review, and reassessment, they get multiple chances to update their Goal agendas over time. But they start with a manageable trio of the most important Goals.

That trio, however, is usually distilled from a much broader array of possible Goals—and we never advise anyone, in these early stages of analysis, against generating the widest possible agenda of these interim positions. In fact, to help account teams generate multiple Goals, we encourage them to utilize two techniques.

The first is creative team thinking. We're strong proponents of this process, because we believe in the truth of the adage "There's nothing as dangerous as an idea if it's the only one you have." Working in an account team, you have a perfect opportunity to think creatively and collectively, generating imaginative, synergistic Goals.

The second technique is to extrapolate from the Situation Appraisal Summary—the document we discussed in Chapter 9. In that Summary, we identified thirteen measures of possible account position: three Strategic Players, three Trends, three Opportunities, three Strengths, and your single most significant Vulnerability. Because Goals have to be connected not only to the ends defined in your Charter Statement but also to the current situation, you should use the Situation Appraisal Summary both as a catalyst and as a reality check on possible end results.

In seeking to define realistic Goals, you should consider these thirteen points interactively. The aim is not simply to come up with thirteen distinct end results—that probably wouldn't be realistic, and it would run the risk of overwhelming your team with agenda items—but to define a handful of "best-bet" Goals that incorporate as many of these critical elements as are feasible.

An ideal Goal incorporates one element of each measure of your position. That is, it uses a unique Strength that can be leveraged through a Strategic Player to capitalize on an Opportunity that rides a growing Trend—while neutralizing your significant Vulnerability. That's a complex scenario, and a difficult one to achieve, but it's still a good benchmark to aim for. At minimum, each of your Goals should meet the criteria set in the "formula" we gave earlier in the chapter. It should show how one of your Strengths will help the Field of Play (or a Strategic Player) to realize an Opportunity—and thus understand how you have contributed to the Large Account's success.

Reality-Checking Your Goals

To summarize this chapter, Goals, as we define them in LAMP analysis, are usually *qualitative* rather than quantitative, will probably take a year or more to achieve, and are best stated from the *account's* point of view. That's the baseline. Once you've met this baseline, we recommend that your team checks whether your suggested Goals are realistically achievable by measuring each one against the following questions:

- Does this Goal align with the Field of Play's mission and immediate needs?
- Does it help to further the achievement of a specific Opportunity, as defined by the Field of Play?
- Which of our strategic Strengths will be brought to bear on the accomplishment of this Goal? Which Opportunity will that Strength help to address?
- Is this Goal realistically achievable in the next several months, given our current position(s) on the Buy-Sell Hierarchy? If it's achieved, will our position improve, or at least remain secure, if that's where we want it to be?
- Which Strategic Player(s) will feel that we have served their best interests if this Goal is accomplished?
- How will accomplishing this Goal help to actualize our Charter Statement?
- Is the Goal written in language that the Field of Play understands?

Testing your supposed "goals" against these guidelines should help you sort out the real (and realistic) positions your company wishes to achieve from the mere "quick fixes" and the pipe dreams. But one final test—which is implied by the final question—is even more rigorous. It goes back to what we've said about involving the customer. After you've written down your Goal in black and white, *show it to the Strategic Players in your Field of Play*. If it's a valid Goal, they'll not only understand it, but buy into it.

In many cases, our clients tell us, when they bring a set of Goals to a Large Account, people in the account will help them tweak the wording, so that it more accurately reflects the emerging relationship. In other cases, account teams gain useful information by asking their clients, "If we are to have a successful relationship with you based on providing real value, what will we have to bring to your organization?" Both of these cases are examples of true collaboration—and they provide the best single test you can get about the realism of your Goals.

Recall our discussion of the account team that set a Goal to improve General Aviation's quality control. If they had showed the first draft of that Goal to the account, it's unlikely that decision makers there would have gotten behind it: The account's own self-interest wasn't clearly stated. The second draft might have gotten them interested, and the third almost certainly would have. It stated bluntly exactly how the seller wanted to be perceived and what it was going to do to bring that about. It would make perfect sense to show this third statement to the customer: Its "partnership" intention was undeniable.

Of course, once it was shown the statement, General Aviation might still have been skeptical, and with good reason: Seeing a mutually beneficial Goal clearly doesn't guarantee you're going to achieve it. But the customer could hardly have responded with "We don't like this idea" or "This seems like a bad place for you to be." The intention was too solid, for both parties. And that's what Goals are, after all: *intended* positions. Like any other position in LAMP strategy, they need the endorsement of the customer to become reality.

In the best of worlds, that endorsement by the account is a public one. Not necessarily a full-page announcement in the *Wall Street Journal* or *Financial Times*, but public enough so that other people in the Large Account—and people in the wider business community—become aware that you have contributed significantly to the growing relationship. A truly effective Goal does more than deliver a knockout benefit to the Large Account. It also so impresses that account that its Strategic Players are willing to serve as references for your business, and to describe both internally and externally how your Strengths have contributed to the achievement of their Opportunity.

This won't always happen automatically. Often, once you've delivered a Goal, you need to actively advertise or "merchandise" it within the Large Account, so that all the players understand what you have done, and your company gets the credit for addressing their Opportunity. The Large Account can provide that credit in a variety of ways, from acknowledging you at national meetings or in speeches, to mentioning your contribution in press interviews, to placing appreciative success stories on its Web site or in its employee newsletter. The specific format is less important than the fact of recognition.

What it all comes down to is Win-Win. LAMP is based on the premise that effective account management requires serving the customer's interests, solving the customer's problems—but not as an altruistic "freebie" or at the expense of your own. If you help the Large Account to Win, you've got to Win too, and one way that this can happen is to have the people in the account acknowledge your contribution. If they're not willing to do this, you may not have provided the value you intended to—or the Large Account may be less interested in a mutually profitable relationship than you had hoped it was. In either case, your account team needs to reassess the situation.

We'll move now from Goals to the specific, incremental investments that can make them a reality.

CHAPTER 12

Focus Investments

"If you focus only on investments that will bring value to the customer, you'll build real business, and you'll avoid the common trap of pushing things that are nice to sell but impossible to deliver."

—Ben Vreeburg,
Sales Director, Loders Croklaan

THE NEXT ELEMENT OF LAMP ANALYSIS, FOCUS INVESTMENTS, ILLUS-trates why the systematic management of limited resources is such a critical factor in Large Account success, and why doing so effectively is essential to achieving your Goals. In line with this understanding, we define Focus Investments as "the concentration of resources directly related to achieving one or more of your Goals and thus of improving your position with the Field of Play."

In stressing the importance of resource management, we're reiterating a point we made in Chapter 1: the fact that today's most successful account managers must function to a great extent like business unit managers, with much of the control and P&L responsibility of those senior people. "Large Account management," as we said earlier, "is becoming a senior management function, driven by executive vision and appropriate resource allocation devoted to building relationships." The success of these newly empowered account managers is determined to a great extent by how wisely they and their teams deploy their organizations' capabilities in Focus Investments.

Precisely because resources are limited, wise Focus Investment means making choices from among a wide array of activities that could be performed, and all of which might have good arguments (and vocal champions) in their favor. *Every resource allocation, therefore, is a resource competition.* This principle operates with equal force whether you're performing Large Account selection in general, determining which Goals are most appropriate for a given Field of Play, or selecting the activities that are designed to achieve those Goals.

One obvious reason that this is true is shortage of time. Even if you had no social or family life and spent every waking hour doing business, you'd still be unable to devote all your time to actualizing a single relation-building activity—and such a single-minded focus wouldn't be effective, anyway. Resources other than time are also limited. If you could devote unlimited funds, support services, and personnel to nailing down the single most significant Goal A for your Field of Play, you might reach that Goal in record time. But the rest of your business—or, if you're an account team, your Large Account—would be struggling as a consequence.

When we speak about resource concentration, therefore, we don't mean tunnel-vision devotion, but rather the relative and judicious focusing of multiple efforts. To stay alive while you're getting to your Goals, you've got to spread your resources optimally over various activities. You've also got to be able, as you choose to invest in Activity A, to reconcile yourself to *not* investing in Activity B. This is seldom easy, and it often involves heated internal competition. If you decide to assign a dedicated IT professional to a given Large Account, that person's time and expertise are going to become unavailable to other accounts. If you identify development of the Asian sector as your top geographical priority, Latin America becomes by definition a lesser priority.

Whoever decides how the pie is to be cut, everybody knows it's not infinitely expandable. If the decision is yours, you need clear reasons for cutting at Point A rather than Point B. And if someone else makes the decisions that affect your bailiwick, it's all the more important to have a well-defined business case to show that person the wisdom of supporting your efforts—the specific efforts you're choosing rather than others.

In this and the following chapter, we'll present some guidelines for making these often difficult investment choices. Let's begin with a very general observation about activities. As your team starts to consider investment decisions, they may find it useful to measure proposed activities against two parameters: their value to the customer or the Field of Play, and whether or not the activities are currently being performed. As indicated in the matrix below, this means that your team basically has four types of activities to consider—with each one calling for a fairly obvious response.

	Not Currently Being Performed	Currently Being Performed
Customer Value	Start	Continue
No Customer Value	Don't Start	Stop

- If the activity has real customer value and you're not currently performing it, *start* it.
- If the activity has real customer value and you're already performing it, *continue* it.
- If the activity has no customer value and you're not currently performing it, *don't start*.
- If the activity has no customer value and you are performing it, *stop*.

These are logical and reliable guidelines, but they're general. Let's get more specific about Focus Investment criteria.

Criteria for Focus Investments

When a market investor considers which mix of securities she wants in her portfolio, she asks this question: "From which of the available investment opportunities am I most likely to get a high, balanced return over a long period of time?" In answering that question, she considers such criteria as current stock prices, past performance, and market trends. Rather than guessing like a lottery or roulette player, she makes an informed wager, trying to minimize her uncertainty, and thus her risk.

That's the smart way to do it, and every Large Account management team ought to employ a similar reasoning process. Unfortunately, many of them, in determining where to place their companies' limited resources, behave not like savvy investors (thinking long-term position) but like day trippers to Las Vegas (thinking short-term gains). Realizing that their available funds are limited, they attempt to cover as many "opportunities" as possible by placing little bets on a dozen different numbers. Occasionally they guess right and go home winners. Usually they get just as flattened by the odds as the person who plays hunches on numbers 7, 14, and 29.

Playing your hunches about which account activities will pay off—or, even worse, spreading your people paper-thin over *every* conceivable path to achieve your Goals—is merely a variation on the theme of "I'm guessing." And account management is too important to be left to guesswork.

Here's the sad part of the scenario. You don't *have* to rely on guesswork to make your choices. Unlike the gambler, you have information that allows you to reduce the risk of the resource investments you make. Not to eliminate it—it's not a perfect world—but certainly to make judicious allocations.

We're referring to the account information that you developed in the Situation Appraisal. There you identified five key strategy elements: Strategic Players, Trends, Opportunities, strategic Strengths, and Vulnerability. As your team begins to make the difficult choices about where to allocate your limited resources, we recommend that you look hard at these five elements and consider the following questions:

- In order to accomplish our Goals, on what Strategic Players do we need to focus our time and efforts?
- In the Field of Play we're looking at, are there specific processes that are "broken" or in need of expert intervention? Which of our Strengths might be leveraged against these processes?
- Do any of the Trends in the Field of Play's environment suggest an investment that might help to enhance our position?
- Of the Opportunities we've identified for this Field of Play, which ones most warrant Focus Investment because of their long-term payoff potential? Which of our Strengths might best address these Opportunities?
- Is there an area in which a focused investment of our resources might help to neutralize or reduce the impact of our Vulnerability?
- Are the investments we're *already* making in the account worthwhile? Has the Large Account confirmed that they're bringing it value?

Focus Investments: Some Real-World Examples

Let's consider a few examples of how Focus Investment works in practice. The first is from the electronics company that we first mentioned in the chapter on Charter Statements—the firm that was targeting a manufacturer's quality control department. One Goal that the account team defined was "To be seen by the Aerospace Division as the supplier that brought them greater quality control reliability by upgrading their patchwork in-house system with a unified systems approach." In moving toward that Goal, the team discovered that the U.S. Navy had recently become this company's own largest customer. Putting the quality control and Navy information together, the account team came up with these two Focus Investments:

- Provide them with better quality control process and measures.
- Help them focus better on how to sell to the Navy.

Notice that neither of these two Focus Investments tied in directly with immediate revenue objectives. Each one, though, did relate directly to the achievement of the Goal that the team had identified.

A second example comes from a packaging company's strategy for improving its relationship with a regional grocery chain. In its Charter Statement, the packager's team had focused its attention on "distinctive packaging that increases the sales of in-store-produced bakery products"—the team was seeking to boost the chain's market share against that of such national giants as Pillsbury and Nabisco. As for Goals, it wanted to achieve two things: "Be recognized as the dominant supplier of eye-catching, innovative packaging that boosts in-store bakery sales." And, because it was poorly positioned with top management, "Get the regional marketing headquarters to understand that we consider them our most important client."

To make optimal use of its resources toward these Goals, the team decided on the following Focus Investments:

1. Invest in a dedicated artistic resource for the Field of Play.
2. Strengthen our position with their marketing department.
3. Build executive level (peer-to-peer) relationships.

Again, none of these Focus Investments related directly to individual pieces of business. But they all related, very clearly, to the business at large, and to the growing *relationship* between the two firms. They also tied in well to our suggested criteria.

- Decisions 1 and 2 played from a *Strength* (the packager's expertise in visual display). They also rode the *Opportunity* of the grocery chain's interest in expanding market share.
- Decision 3 sought to neutralize the *Vulnerability* of poor positioning by developing *Strategic Player* contacts up the hierarchy.

For a final example, let's consider the Focus Investments that Pat Murphy's PreComm team came up with in seeking to improve its relationship with the Datavoc European division. Here are the Goals that the team decided on:

- Be seen by Alan Coates as the supplier on whom he could rely for components with good reliability and minimum Dead on Arrivals.
- Be acknowledged by procurement as the vendor with the best performance in terms of flexibility and just-in-time delivery.
- Be acknowledged by Heather Rist to Dave Kaufman as the supplier that offers best whole-life component costs versus unit base price.
- Be seen by Dave Kaufman as having done enough to reverse the damage done by our negation of the design agreement.
- Be recommended by Pete Sanchez to Mark Duval as the expert design partner for the next family of Datavoc's air-conditioning controller units.
- Be seen by Datavoc's European Manufacturing board as the supplier who helped them consistently control costs.

Here are the Focus Investment decisions that the team determined would help them realize these Goals:

- Reestablish a mutually satisfactory design agreement.
- Become indispensable to their new product design process.

- Ensure that Datavoc will get timely, cost-effective delivery.
- Demonstrate our reliability with statistics.
- Demonstrate the impact of product failures on brand choice.
- Show that our "higher" unit cost actually translates into a lower lifetime cost of ownership.

As with the other examples, you can see how the team believes that these investment decisions might help to accomplish their stated Goals. The first two Focus Investments relate directly to PreComm's intention of becoming Datavoc's premier design partner—something of particular interest to the manufacturer's engineering design manager, Mark Duval. The third and fourth items address Datavoc's desire for delivery of less expensive components on a predictable schedule—with a minimum of DOAs. The fifth relates that concern to Datavoc's broader interest in securing its brand position against both European and Asian competitors. The final item addresses the crucial cost issue—a sensitive matter for Datavoc procurement, where much of the data will reside but where there is pressure to keep PreComm down at commodity level. In all of these cases, then, the Focus Investments utilize PreComm Strengths to improve the perceptions (the "be seen as" factors) of Strategic Players in the Field of Play.

Investing in the Future

You've probably noticed one feature common to all these Focus Investment examples. Not one of them was cheap. They were initially free to the customers, but they all cost the investing companies heavily, in real time and real dollars. That means, to some degree, that they were painful. Many companies are reluctant to take on this kind of pain. They'd rather minimize the outlay of Focus Investments in the hope that hard work and a little luck will pay off. In some part of the account. Somehow. Sometime.

Like a portfolio strategy built exclusively on risk avoidance, this is shortsighted, and it almost never pays off in good business. It may seem more comfortable, less expensive, or less anxiety-provoking in the short run. But in a highly competitive atmosphere, the failure to focus your resources on your best opportunities for building the relationship inevitably leaves you open to account "drift," to competitive attack, and to the uncertainties of a "strategy" built on chance.

Focus Investments are not guarantees. And we admit that they can be expensive. Expanding your consulting services, hiring a top-notch artist, sending your executives out to call on theirs—none of that is cheap. It's not cheap to buy a blue-chip stock either. You do so for a good strategic reason. Not because there's no risk of losing money. But because, considering all the available information, the probability that your investments will give you a good return down the line is a lot higher with a proven stock than at a gambling casino.

Success is not guaranteed. But as today's account management leaders all know, just as you've got to spend money to make money, you've got to invest resources in order to realize a return. And one thing *is* guaranteed. If you choose to spread your resources thin rather than focusing them, you're taking a far bigger gamble with your Large Account's health than you'd be taking with even the riskiest of Focus Investments.

CHAPTER **13**

Stop Investments

*"When you decide to spend more money in one area because
it's important, you generally have to get it from somewhere else.
That's not canceling something, it's rebalancing.
Successful companies do it every day."*

—Jerry Barnes, Sales Consultant, Miller Heiman

THE FOCUS INVESTMENT PRINCIPLE HELPS YOUR TEAM IDENTIFY THOSE
activities where dedicating your time, personnel, and other resources will bring you closer to the achievement of your Goals.
The flip side of Focus Investment is what we call Stop Investment. It helps you to identify those areas in which your current resource investment is not paying off—and to work in
conjunction with the Field of Play to cut back in those areas.
The two principles operate together; interactively they function as a best practice of resource allocation.

Few of our clients ever question the wisdom of Focus Investment. But Stop Investment is a harder pill to swallow, and it
frequently encounters staunch and articulate resistance. This
resistance derives from some firmly entrenched articles of the
corporate canon. One is the old cliché that customers are always right (and therefore that you should do anything they
ask you to do, even if you Lose by doing so). Another is the
fear of boat rocking: the belief that anytime you introduce a
change into a basically steady relationship, you risk damaging

it. A third is that, in order to build business, you should consider responding to *every* request for proposal, and fight for every piece of business as if it meant your survival. These ideas have a common premise: In serving customers, more is better, and the company that throws unlimited resources at all of its good opportunities has a distinct competitive advantage over resource-constrained rivals.

It sounds plausible. And maybe in the world of economic formulas, it works out. But in the real world, this conventional belief spells disaster.

We've asked hundreds of colleagues a simple question: "How often have you written solid business from an RFP that came in at the last minute?" The responses have ranged from "One time in a thousand" to "Never." To anyone who understands account management, these are predictable responses. In our gut we know all requests are not alike. We know that when customers ask us to deliver a proposal in two days, they've already decided on another vendor and are rounding up last-minute alternatives to show their finance departments they've shopped around. We know that responding to a request for a proposal in these conditions has almost no chance of landing durable business.

We also know about the leads that *do* bring in business, but the kind of business you later wish you'd never written. We've all run into those "irresistible" major orders where the post-transaction costs in service and damage control turn what once looked like a great revenue stream into a dry creek bed. If you've ever had the pleasure of managing an account whose key players are never satisfied, who continually hold their suppliers up for ransom, whose needs grow exponentially as your resources grow arithmetically, you'll understand what we mean when we say that some Large Account business is more trouble than it is worth. That's one reason, in fact, that we advised you in Chapter 2 to be careful about selecting an account for LAMP strategy, and to consider not just potential revenue, but mutuality of value.

This is where Stop Investment comes in. Our advice for how

to deal with obviously marginal business, potentially deadly "opportunities," or fatally high-maintenance accounts is simple: *Don't.* Let your competition have those thrills. Because your energy and your resources are both finite, focus them where they have a decent chance of paying off. If that chance is merely fair, think about stopping further investment. If it's two steps away from never, *just say no.*

Identifying Stop Investment Candidates

How do you recognize activities that you should consider candidates for Stop Investment? We'll give you some exemplary scenarios, but first, here are some general principles that operate in virtually all scenarios. If you've been investing in an account-support activity, or are considering doing so, and aren't sure about the payoff potential, ask yourselves these three testing questions:

- Is this activity justified given the *value* it is bringing to the Field of Play?
- Do we have evidence that the Strategic Players *acknowledge* this value? Have they told us, in so many words, that they endorse the activity?
- Is this activity clearly and significantly helping us to accomplish one or more of our *Goals*?

If the answers to these questions are negative or uncertain, you may be investing too heavily (or inappropriately) in a given situation. And this may or may not relate to such obvious "misinvestments" as following up a low-quality lead or answering an unreasonable request for account support. The concept of Stop Investment refers to *any* business situation where you've been dedicating time, effort, people, or other resources, and the investment, as your team calculates it, is not paying off.

Stop Investment doesn't mean you should cut and run at the first sign of diminishing or low returns. Investments in a relationship, just like cash investments in a stock portfolio, can take time to mature, so sometimes even when things seem a bit unbalanced—that is, when you're putting more into the account than you're getting in return—it still makes strategic sense to keep building the relationship. But at other times the account "opportunity" is so littered with danger signals that not pulling out becomes an affront to rationality. To give you some specific examples, we advise you to consider reallocating your resources whenever you encounter one or more of the following scenarios:

1. You're on the outside track. That is, your competition has the inside track, and no matter how diligently you pursue the relationship, you're always two steps behind. Perhaps your competition has a unique Strength that you can't match, or your own Strengths are irrelevant to the customer, or the competition has been long entrenched in the account. Yes, you should go head to head with your competitors, but only when there's a reasonable chance of good return. Keeping a presence in the account is one thing; pouring endless resources against an entrenched opponent is quite another.

2. It's not your real business. A friend of ours is a cabinet-maker who creates period reproductions for a chain of hotels. Recently one hotel manager asked him to do some small remodeling jobs as well. Our friend is capable of performing that work, but it's not his area of expertise, and every hour he spends on a minor trim job is time taken away from his specialty—and therefore from the completion of high-yield projects. On our advice he explained to the manager that he was not in the remodeling business. He would have to decline such requests in the future but would be happy to recommend a handyman whose skills were top-notch. The manager couldn't really argue, because she ended up with first-rate work in *both* areas. The lesson: Define the business you want to compete in, and do the best work you can in that field. If you've broadened your efforts to a relatively unknown field and they're draining your resources from more profitable business, it may be time to Stop Investment in this field and "get back to the knitting."

3. You're flying blind. You can't sell or manage effectively in an information vacuum. Therefore, if you feel, for *whatever* reason, that you lack sufficient information about the impact your efforts are having in a Large Account, it may be time to stop and reexamine the activities you've been focusing on. If you're feeling your way, if you "need more data," if there have been multiple "surprises" in handling this business, those are Red Flags that should make you wary of getting in deeper. We don't mean for you to pull back the minute you draw a blank. Obviously the first step to take when you lack information is to try to get that information; LAMP analysis is specifically designed to help you do that. But if repeated attempts to read the account leave you in the dark—if, for example, after a month or so you still haven't been able to draft a clear Charter Statement or identify active Sponsors or Strategic Coaches—then this may not be the optimal time to pursue a deeper relationship in this Field of Play.

4. Time and money pits. A Hollywood comedy called *The Money Pit* describes the misadventures of a couple whose new house, constantly in need of repair, eats their bank account like a black hole eats light. In business it's not funny. A mining firm once received a court order to clean up the toxic waste from a lake it had fouled; rather than spend the $2 million the cleanup would have cost, it hired a raft of environmental lawyers—and spent ten times that much in legal fees. We've all had similar—if not quite so severe—money and time sinks in our Large Accounts. The worst ones are prime candidates for Stop Investment. As a rule of thumb, we recommend cutting any project or activity that has already cost you *two to three* times its original cost estimate.

These four scenarios are not the only Stop Investment candidates you can run into, and running into them doesn't mean, automatically, that you've got to pull out immediately or lose your shirt. But they are reliable signals to the savvy investor that it may be time to cut your losses and say philosophically, "It seemed like a good idea when we started it."

"Never Say Die": Four Versions

It's not easy to get this idea across. In our programs, the concept of Stop Investment generates more controversy, and more resistance, than any other. The fact is that most account managers, and most businesses, don't like the idea of pulling back. They resist it usually for four related reasons.

The first one is the sales professional's perennial optimism. As salespeople and as account managers we're ingrained with the old idea that a "positive attitude" and "hard work" can work miracles. They can, of course, if they're combined with a rigorous attention to the customer's needs, sound account analysis, and good strategy. But without those pragmatic elements of account management, a gung ho attitude will get you just about as far as a shoeshine and a smile. Yet the attitude persists. With it goes the self-destructive belief that if you keep plugging away at a piece of business, or an account relationship, eventually everything will turn your way.

Second is the bread-on-the-waters delusion. For many companies, the standard method of developing account business is the old broadcast method: Scatter your seeds and hope that one out of a hundred turns into a tree. Fine for Johnny Appleseed, but not for business. The idea behind this "philosophy" is that you can't really tell good account opportunities from bad ones, and you shouldn't try. Just keep throwing everything you have in the customer's lap, and eventually he's bound to find something that he considers of value.

The third version of "Never say die" is "We're already committed, so let's push on." For example: We've already sunk thirty grand into the Green Springs development project. Rather than admitting that this investment was a mistake, let's sink thirty more. Eventually it will all come back. Besides, if we pull out now, our standing with the account will suffer as a consequence. This combination of stubbornness and gambler's delirium saps the strength of countless businesses every day.

Finally, we hear from our clients that, as much as they'd *like* to kill an unprofitable area of account activity, they're often blocked from doing so by senior management. There's no doubt that this is a major impediment to Stop Investments. Once a marketing objective is enshrined in one of those twenty-pound, holy-writ account plans, it becomes "sanctified" by management approval and in many cases becomes part of the CEO's pet marketing scheme—not infrequently because it represents something that worked for him before he became the CEO. It takes fortitude to buck that kind of entrenchment.

A few years ago, for example, we did some consulting with a Midwestern food service company whose third largest account was a manufacturing giant. The food service firm ran the cafeteria operations of six separate factories of the manufacturer, and lost money, every year, on every one. This seemed like an obvious candidate for Stop Investment. Yet when we suggested that the food service company should reconsider the wisdom of holding on to that account, we were told that it was the founder's pride and joy—the first Fortune 500 account that he had nailed down himself years ago. Pulling out might have been judicious, but politically it was virtually impossible.

The Hard Fact of Triage

We answer all these versions of the "Never say die" argument with the same commonsense observation: *All business is not alike.* Nor are all the activities that you perform, or could perform, to position your company more effectively in a Large Account. An underlying principle of the entire LAMP program is that some accounts have more potential than others, and should be managed accordingly. That works on a micro level, too. Some activities that you perform for your major accounts, some Focus Investments, have more potential than others for getting you to your Goals. Since your Goals are designed to benefit the account, this also means that some investments bring more value to the account than others do; not everything you do is necessarily worth saving.

Because your resources are limited, this means that *some projects must die.* To use a gruesome but accurate analogy, you've got to perform a kind of triage on your Large Accounts and on the activities that you're performing within them. You've got to decide (1) which activities deserve your immediate and full support, (2) which ones can survive for a while without aggressive management, and (3) which ones are lost causes, bleeding you dry. And you need the courage to *walk away* from this third group.

We don't mean "Walk away and let George take over." That's just passing the buck. If the Baton Rouge plant of the Harrow account has become a money sink, it won't suddenly turn into a cash cow because a different rep, or a different department, is doing your work. When we say drop it, we mean just that: Commit, as a *company,* to pulling out. You can hang on if there's a *reasonable* expectation of future success, but if the chance is one in a hundred, give it up. Nursing Baton Rouge through a five-year death struggle means ignoring other, more salvageable opportunities. It's the hardest lesson the battlefield medic has to learn: Spending an hour with the guy who's almost gone loses him *and the ones who might have been saved.* Recognizing this grim reality is a necessary part of being a professional, in medicine *and* in business.

Stop Investment: The Hidden Benefits

The military analogy isn't exact. In fact, letting a low-potential activity "die" seldom has a negative impact on the customer, and it almost always improves your company's strategic leverage. Some examples show why.

Consider first our electronics company. Recall that one of its Focus Investments was to hire a former account sales manager to learn how the account sold to *its* largest account, the U.S. Navy. One Stop Investment that the team defined was to "cease pursuing sales with low potential in the customer's *non*-Navy-related business." That's Stop and Focus Investments working together. The team made a conscious decision to *redirect* company resources from low-potential to high-potential activities. You could say that the company "lost" the non-Navy business, but what it really lost was the aggravation that went with it. What it gained was a better position—and at no extra cost to either organization.

Here's a second example. A nationwide trucking company once totally reassessed its marketing strategy. After analyzing figures from dozens of terminals and regional markets, account executives came to a sobering realization. Over one thousand of their accounts were losing concerns; the revenues they brought in didn't even match operating expenses. Faced with this discovery, company managers called the sales force together and asked them to present a hard choice to their accounts. They were to acknowledge flatly "We can't continue to provide you quality service at current prices. Here's what we *can* offer you." And they were to present three options. "One, we can increase your rates. Two, we can change the mix of your business so we carry your high-yield loads as well as the low-yield ones we're carrying now; with a new mix, we can guarantee your rates *and* our quality. Three, we can shake hands and say good-bye."

Virtually all of the trucker's customers appreciated the supplier's candor. And over 80 percent of them elected to stay on board, with the altered mix that would make them profitable accounts as well as guarantee them continued service. Far from alienating business by presenting Stop Investment as an option, the trucking company actually strengthened its hold and served the long-term needs of both its customers *and* itself.

For a final example, consider PreComm. In assessing how best to allocate their limited resources to the Datavoc account's needs, Pat Murphy's team identifies two areas in which current resources might best be redirected elsewhere. The first relates to design. Recall from the previous chapter that one of the team's Focus Investments was to establish a new, mutually satisfactory, design agreement. So it's appropriate that one of their two Stop Investments is to "stop free design collaboration." There's no point in continuing to provide free consulting in this area as the particulars of the new arrangement are being worked out. This is obviously a Stop Investment that has to be done in consultation with the account's Strategic Players;

given the potential long-term benefit to Datavoc, they agree it should be done.

The second Stop Investment that Murphy's team identifies is also an example of resource redirection. As part of his corporate-wide responsibility, Murphy has been managing not just the Datavoc account, but also a smaller account based in New York. He suggests, and the team agrees, that he should assign that smaller account to another PreComm manager, so he will be able to devote his full attention to growing the Datavoc business. In terms of PreComm business as a whole, this shifts rather than drops attention from the smaller account. But in terms of the Datavoc accounts, it's clearly a Stop Investment—one that will free up the resource, Pat Murphy's attention, that is needed to support the Focus Investments the team had identified.

As these examples make clear, there are basically three related benefits of carefully considered Stop Investments:

- By plugging the time and money drain, they help you *conserve* resources that poor investment strategy always wastes.
- They free up resources that can be used in better ways. They allow you to *redirect* your time and resources for more predictable results.
- If used intelligently, they can *consolidate* your position with valued customers by showing them that you are ready to serve their interests in those areas, and *only* in those areas, where you can do it best.

Resource Investment: A Team Approach

In LAMP analysis, you use Focus Investment and Stop Investment interactively to optimize the value of your resource allocations, and to ensure that they're bringing you closer to realizing your Goals. This process should be conducted by the account team collaboratively, and the results should be presented to and approved by two "authorities"—your own senior management and the Field of Play.

Getting senior approval for a "pulled" investment is important because, without it, the decision might easily be questioned and the strategy thus endangered. Experian Sales Director Neville Seabridge speaks from personal experience on this point. "If I wanted to pull resources away from a marginally profitable client," he says, "and I didn't clear it with our CEO, that client could easily pick up the phone and get the strategically sound but unpopular decision overturned. That would undo all the good work the account team did, and leave everyone, including the client, looking at a Lose. That's why a Stop Investment is something that the entire organization, top to bottom, must buy into."

The reason you also have to share potential Stop Investments with the customer is implicit in Seabridge's comment. If you pull resources from an account or an account initiative without first consulting the party most affected, you're saying, in effect, "Your opinion doesn't matter to us." Stop Investments can often be "sold" to such customers as in their best long-term interest. But only if you involve them in the decision up front.

With those two provisos in mind, here's an overview of the steps through which an analysis of Focus and Stop Investments should proceed.

Step 1: Focus Investments. First, using all the information gathered together so far, the team identifies the areas where your organization should concentrate its resources with regard to this Large Account *over the next one to three years.* In doing this, it may help to tie potential Focus Investments into one or more of the Situation Appraisal elements. As a team, ask yourselves:

• What activities can we perform that would highlight for the customer the uniqueness of our *Strengths?* Are we sure that this Field of Play even understands our uniqueness? Because the best product in the world won't sell itself, do we need to focus more effort on demonstrating our uniqueness to the customer? If we're well positioned in the customer's organizational hierarchy, can we do more to capitalize on that Strength? Are we protecting our Strengths aggressively enough, or do we need to shield them from potential erosion?

• Which *Opportunities* that the Large Account is considering warrant extended resource investment on our part because of their long-term payoff potential? Look not only for business that will pay off for the customer today, or this year, but for Opportunities that you can help them grow over time. Are there elements of this customer's business that are in their infancy now, but that might provide them solid revenue or competitive advantage in the future?

• The same question should be asked on the macro level. What company-related, industry-related, and broad market *Trends* suggest a more dedicated focus of our efforts? What's happening with this Large Account internally? Are there changes that we can turn to their advantage by a more focused or increased effort? Externally, are there Trends on the horizon that could damage them unless we anticipate their impact?

• Can we strengthen our position with one or more *Strategic Players* by the careful use of a Focus Investment? What value will they see in this investment, and how do we know that they will see this value? Investigate Anti-Sponsors as well as Sponsors and Strategic Coaches. Neutralizing an enemy by spending time and effort on that person can be just as valuable a contribution to your strategy as nurturing an already good relationship.

• Does our major *Vulnerability* suggest an area that needs to be "backfilled" with more selling time, support time, or other resources? In other words, do we have this weakness because we've been neglecting activities we *should* have been performing? How can we use our Strengths and Strategic Players to leverage a Focus Investment against it?

Once your team has identified a half-dozen or so possible Focus Investments, we recommend that you reach a consensus on the *two or three* most important ones. Then test the validity of these choices by asking yourself three more questions:

• Will following through on this Focus Investment clearly contribute to the achievement of our Goals? In what way, specifically, will it change the way we are seen by the Strategic Players? Will that changed perception translate into an enhanced understanding of our Strengths—or will it minimize the perception of our Vulnerability?

• Will following through on this Focus Investment strengthen our present *position* in the account? Will it reduce our uncertainty about how the account operates? Improve our relationship with one or more Strategic Players? Help us get a better foothold on where we want to be on the Buy-Sell Hierarchy? Again, you don't need to prove the link in a mathematical formula. But you should be able to state it clearly, to the satisfaction of everyone on your team.

• Is there *value* in this Focus Investment for the Field of Play? Have they acknowledged and endorsed the activity?

Step 2: Stop Investments. Next the account team performs the less comfortable, but equally necessary, flip side of time investment strategy by getting rid of those activities that won't pay off. Whether they jump out at you or not, they *always* exist. To bring them to the surface, have your team ask the following:

• What activities are we involved in where we lack a unique Strength advantage, or where that advantage is not clear to the Field of Play? Good strategy always starts from Strength: If your competitor has an inside track in a given area, it may be best to leave that area to him or her for the time being and compete where you're stronger.

• Are we not expert in any portion of the Large Account we're targeting? Do we lack the experience to compete effectively in any portion? Is there any area where what we're being asked to do is drawing valuable resources away from areas in which we can perform better? Are we operating to maximum effect in our own defined market, or have we gotten too far away from the knitting?

• In what areas are we flying blind? Where, in spite of all our information gathering, are we still feeling our way, without sufficient data? Where have there been a lot of surprises, mostly negative in impact? When is it time to recognize the poor return and cut our losses?

• Are we trying to sell a new product, or an old product into a new market? The best product in the world hasn't got a chance if the timing of market entry is premature. Are there areas where we should step back, let the competition take the heat for "opening" this slice of Large Account business, and consider reinvesting at a later time?

• What activity or project has been a time and money sink? Where have we been throwing good money after bad—and good time after bad—for too long? Although there's no hard and fast rule for identifying such black holes, remember our suggested rule of thumb: If you've gone two to three times over the original estimate, no matter how good the business *could* be, you may already have paid too much up front.

When you've uncovered areas of possible Stop Investment, you should agree on the *two* areas that are doing you the most harm. Write them down and commit, as a team, to squander no more resources in that direction. If you can identify more than two investments that should be dropped, fine. But two is the minimum.

Step 3: Rebalance the focus. Finally, make an informed estimate of how much time (or money, effort, or other resources) your company is likely to *save* by eliminating these two dropped investments. Develop a consensus reaction about the *increased* investment opportunities that are now open to you with the elimination of the time and money drains. Where does it make sense to *rebalance* this newly available company resource? Look at your Focus Investment choices once again. How does the release of formerly locked-up resources affect them? Does the investment freed up from Stop Investments suggest *other* Focus Investments—ones you may have considered too costly up to now? Revise your Focus Investment list as your team sees fit, based on the new allocation of resources.

In performing this last step, many of our clients find it helpful to quantify—that is, to numerically estimate the resource savings involved—and to use the estimated figures in assessing potential benefits. We encourage them to write down, in as much detail as possible, the following information:

- The current or projected *cost* of each Focus Investment, in terms of money, time, personnel, or other resources.
- The projected *savings*, in terms of the same parameters, of each Stop Investment.
- The *time frame* for each Focus Investment: when it will start and how long it will continue.
- The planned *stop date* for each Stop Investment.
- The potential *impact* on the relationship with the Field of Play of each Focus Investment and each Stop Investment.

The final item here is a qualitative one, and we include it to guard against the tendency to reduce everything to numbers. But some degree of quantification is not only helpful, but a necessary balancing factor as you draft a LAMP strategy. Measuring how much your activities are costing your company, in terms of real dollars or euros or yen, helps an account team understand the practical element in relationship building, an element that has to be tested, at the end of the day, on your company's balance sheets.

Newcomers to LAMP sometimes imagine that, in touting perception and position and B2B relationships, we are slighting or forgetting the importance of making the numbers come out— that is, of having companies that perform LAMP analysis show a profit. Nothing could be further from the truth. In fact, as longtime champions of the Win-Win philosophy, we insist that, as you achieve your Goals and become better positioned in your Large Account's eyes, you get both qualitative *and* quantitative recognition for that achievement. We insist, in other words, that you get paid for your efforts. We'll elaborate on this point in the following chapter.

CHAPTER 14

Revenue Targets

"Money speaks sense in a language all nations understand."

—Aphra Behn

WE'VE BEEN STRESSING THAT GOOD ACCOUNT RELATIONSHIPS DELIVER *value to the customer*. Every principle we've introduced in this account strategy section—the Charter Statement, Goals, and Focus Investments to secure those Goals—supports this emphasis. It's not going too far to say that the entire point of setting a LAMP strategy is to ensure that your customers—and their customers—realize value.

But value is a two-way street. You don't deliver value to your customers out of altruism, but because you understand that it's the single invariable key to building a long-term relationship. In that relationship, your company must realize value, too, or it will be locked into a Lose-Win scenario. In this chapter, to ensure that your LAMP strategy rests on mutuality, we introduce an element called Revenue Targets. By setting appropriate Revenue Targets as part of your strategy, your team defines the value that *you* will receive when the relationship you are building begins to bear fruit.

We define Revenue Targets as the sales results that your team believes can be achieved in the Field of Play within a specified time frame—usually one to three years out from today. Since most account managers are measured and compensated based on how well they meet such targets, the utility of the Revenue Target concept is pretty obvious. But such targets also serve two additional, related functions.

- First, they enable you to measure the success of the Focus Investments you are making—to "quantify the yield" of those critical and often expensive resource allocations.
- Second, they provide a *business case* to convince members of your own organization—senior management and others who free up resources—that those investments are worth the company's efforts.

To anyone who imagines that LAMP is a "soft" approach to account management—as a skeptical colleague once suggested to us, a "vision thing" rather than a "business thing"—the concept of Revenue Targets provides a useful corrective. It gives you a way to demonstrate that your strategy is literally paying off.

Single Sales Objectives

In discussing Revenue Targets, we counsel our clients to begin with relatively small, individual transactional objectives and then build them out—aggregate them, in effect—to create a broad picture of expected revenue over time. To a degree, of course, that picture will begin with whatever revenue stream you have already established with the Large Account—the expected return that this account brings you and that, in fact, contributes to your seeing it as a Large Account in the first place. Beyond that, though, the picture will likely include additional, incremental revenue that is tied to transactions in progress, or future business that hasn't yet been defined. These smaller, "incremental targets" are what veterans of our Strategic Selling process have come to know as Single Sales Objectives. They are defined the same way in LAMP as they are in Strategic Selling. A Single Sales Objective is:

- Product-, service-, or solution-oriented
- Specific, clear, and concise
- Definable and measurable
- Tied to a timeline
- Truly single (not connected by "and")

By "truly single" we mean that a Single Sales Objective is not an amalgam or a compound of two or more objectives. In our Strategic Selling workshops, we ensure the required "singularity" by saying that, in writing down their objectives, clients should avoid using the connector "and." The other criteria here are fairly self-explanatory, but to illustrate them and to ensure precision, we ask clients to define each Single Sales Objective according to the following formula:

SINGLE SALES OBJECTIVE

To deliver to the ———— (Field of Play)
———— (amount or volume)
of ———— (product, service, or solution)
for ———— (revenue or other units)
by ———— (date).

This formula makes it clear how much a Single Sales Objective differs from a Goal. To a certain degree, Goals are soft: They don't have a hard data component. "Be seen as providing cutting-edge research data to their engineering department"—that's clear enough, and quite specific, but there are no *numbers* involved. Single Sales Objectives, on the other hand, are defined expressly in terms of numbers. As the formula indicates, such a revenue objective states precisely how much of a given product or service you expect to place with your targeted Field of Play by a given date. Thus, whereas Goals are an indication of intended position, Single Sales Objectives—and Revenue Targets—are an indication of intended *volume.*

Here are some examples of Single Sales Objectives that were established by some of our clients' key account teams in LAMP workshops:

- "We'll deliver 150,000 gallons of our Formula TLC to the Ohio plant by the end of fiscal year 2005."
- "The Engineering Division will accept shipment of fifty gross units of the Favax transformer by July 1, 2006."
- "The iZan Group will sign for $3.75 million worth of software licenses by the start of Fall Quarter 2007."

Notice that the measures of volume vary from case to case—you may want to set a Single Sales Objective for one Large Account in terms of dollar or euro revenue and for another in terms of tonnage shipped—but in every case, the volume is expressed numerically. Your company's more mathematically minded people might take a little convincing on the concept of Goals, but they'll take Single Sales Objectives and Revenue Targets as unarguable—what one of our colleagues calls "blinding glimpses of the obvious."

One caveat. Just because a Single Sales Objective defines what you'll be delivering, it doesn't mean that the customer's perception of that deliverable becomes unimportant. On the contrary, the only Revenue Targets that make any sense are those that both you *and* the account perceive as delivering value. This ensures that the payoff you anticipate furthers mutuality.

Beyond Aggregation

Single Sales Objectives serve both as "mini-targets" in themselves and as transactions, projects, or engagements that, as they begin to realize value, are also expected to contribute to your broader Revenue Targets—above and beyond what you're already receiving from the account as an ongoing revenue stream. To a degree, you can define those broader, one-to-three-year targets by "rolling up" all your Single Sales Objectives into an aggregate projection. But there's likely to be more to your Revenue Target than just this accumulation, because the more you work with the account to meet its changing needs, the more business potential is going to be revealed—and you'll discover at least some of this potential in "hidden" areas that may have relatively little to do with your initial revenue objectives.

One of our clients—a large pharmaceutical firm—found this out shortly after the end of a LAMP session. The account team had set an overall annual revenue projection of $200,000 from one of their Fields of Play. They went home from the session not expecting to see much of a revenue kick for about twelve months. But thanks to the analysis that had begun during that session—and to the enhanced relationships that soon evolved with the Strategic Players—by four months down the line they had already uncovered and closed $250,000 worth of business. Only some of that came from Single Sales Objectives that they had identified. A great deal came from business relationship opportunities that, before starting Situation Appraisal, weren't even visible on their radar screens.

That's a fairly common scenario in LAMP analysis, and it points clearly to the fact that, in calculating revenue, the one-to-three-year Revenue Target is often more than the sum of its anticipated components. This is why calculating a Revenue Target effectively is less a matter of counting up "deals" than of speculative forecasting. And this fact can lead to a certain amount of confusion.

Forecasting Revenue: Two Problems

You might think it would be easier to define a hard Revenue Target than a soft Goal like "Be seen as providing cutting-edge research data." Aren't numbers easier to work with than perceptions?

In fact they're not. Revenue Targets are basically sales forecasts, and sales forecasting is a notoriously imprecise process. It's far from easy to set Revenue Targets that are realistic and that at the same time provide the appropriate incentives for people managing accounts. The fact that salespeople and account teams are constantly complaining about their quotas indicates how few companies manage to do this well.

The problems here go beyond the inevitable difference in perspective between the managers who set the quotas and the people who have to meet them. Two scenarios frequently complicate the estimation of how much revenue an account can generate. Both speak to the fissure in many modern organizations between the people out in the trenches and those in the central office.

Scenario 1: The extrapolation trap. In this scenario, rather than performing the kind of meticulous account assessment that our LAMP clients perform in Situation Appraisal, the forecaster looks at last year's figures and jacks them up by a certain percentage. "We did 1.4 million with this account in 2004. We're going for 10 percent growth. So this year's target is going to be 1.54 million." In a perfect example of "rearview mirror" calculation, this gives a Revenue Target that's perfectly quantifiable, but that may bear little relation to account reality.

Last year's figures, after all, are just that—last year's figures. Any number of things might have happened since they were turned in that could undermine, or completely invalidate, the jacked-up projection. The account may now be experiencing internal difficulties that didn't exist a year ago. Overhead or supply costs may have gone up. New market entrants may have made its existing IT solutions obsolete. The firm may be reorganizing, preoccupied with government regulations, or shifting its market focus. In addition, any or all of these things could be happening in *your* company, too. A failure to consider such changes—in other words, a failure to keep your Situation Appraisal up-to-date—can lead to unrealistically high (or low) revenue forecasts.

Scenario 2: "Creative" forecasting. In a second scenario, armchair strategists, working with spreadsheets and formulas, take over from the people in charge of the account and design an attack plan for a nonexistent battlefield. In the *Harvard Business Review,* authors George Day and Liam Fahey once acutely identified the deficiencies of such "creative" forecasting: "The analyst changes one variable at a time, seeing what happens when the market growth is 1 percent higher, when gross margin is 2 percent better, when working capital is cut by $3 million. After several hours of experimenting and testing, the variables become completely disconnected from the original strategy projections."

"Creative" or "projective" forecasts thus become inconsistent not only with each other but with the real world in which the company operates. And the people who are in charge of actually generating the revenue—the marketing, sales, and account teams and their managers—are obliged to turn the analyst's fantasy into reality. Sometimes, by Herculean efforts, they succeed. Often they don't, because the projections are just too blue-sky for anybody's reach.

The common error in both these scenarios isn't just a reliance on numbers crunching. You can't run a business without crunching numbers. The problem is that, in their zeal to quantify everything, many firms forget the obvious: that *the customer's changing needs affect the value of every figure.* If your projections don't hook into your customer's *current* situation, it doesn't matter that you've run a perfect program.

Rationalized Forecasts: Bracketing

To help you avoid such problems, we recommend a calculation technique that we call "bracketing." Because it's often difficult to come up with realistic Revenue Targets, we urge your team to do so in three steps.

First, pick a Primary Revenue Target that you could achieve if your sales and other resources were *unconstrained.* That's *really* blue-sky thinking. We understand that. But identifying what kind of revenue the account might deliver if your organization allowed you to pull out all the stops helps you visualize a kind of "high-ceiling" fantasy that, paradoxically, is usually *less* fantastic than spreadsheet-generated spin. This is useful in providing "stretch" to your projections.

Second, pick an equally fantastic *low* Revenue Target: the lowest figure that, if current resource levels continue over the target period, all members of your team can buy into. In other words, define the *minimum acceptable* revenue.

Finally, look at what's realistic. Come to a consensus on a Revenue Target somewhere between the high and low brackets. Your account team's aim should be to "stretch realistically."

To see how the bracketing technique works out in a real-world situation, let's look at the Revenue Targets that Pat Murphy and his PreComm team come up with as the "payoff" for their Focus Investments. They have determined that the European Manufacturing division of Datavoc is currently spending about $300 million for the various categories of components that PreComm supplies—with about 35 percent of that figure, or $105 million, going to PreComm. The team begins by determining a high, or resource-unconstrained, figure.

Resource-unconstrained here means, for example, that all the Focus Investments they've defined will get rapid management approval, that Robert Glock's new components transfer system will be put in place without a hitch, that the growing relationship will offset Dave Kaufman's resistance to working with Glock, that the survey on consumer attitudes toward product failure will cement Datavoc's desire for reliable components, and that the new design contract that the legal department is drafting will meet with instant approval from their Datavoc counterparts.

The team realizes that's a tall order. But if it all comes through, they calculate that revenue from components supply and paid design services could amount to as much as $200 million annually over the next couple of years. If the design agreement also starts to build in new technologies like VoIP, then that figure could rise significantly. In that scenario, PreComm could more than double its current Datavoc wallet share, plus get a significant return from new products—making the $200 million figure a conservative high-end target.

Next, the team calculates how much revenue PreComm would receive in the next few years if virtually nothing changed in the current account situation. They ask themselves, in other words, "What if none of our Focus Investments comes through? What if we have to continue handling Datavoc the same way we're handling them right now, but with no additional commitment of resources?" They understand that, if that happens—if legal sits on the new contract or Datavoc balks at it, if the customer survey doesn't give the anticipated results, or if Glock's transfer scheme fails and Kaufman continues to mistrust him—then it's unlikely that the anticipated revenue from this account will rise much above the $105 million annually they're getting now.

There's some team discussion about this figure, with Sam Jones suggesting that, as PreComm's own costs rise, "flat growth" like that is "simply unacceptable." Finance head Alicia Carvounis agrees, and after some debate the team agrees to identify $120 million as the low-end Revenue Target. That's the bare minimum that the team, collectively, is willing to settle for, even if none of the support systems they anticipate actually come through.

Finally, the team compares the high- and low-end estimates and the investments needed and reaches a compromise: a midrange estimate of $170 million. That becomes their stated Revenue Target—the income they expect to receive annually over the next three years.

In drafting your own Revenue Target statements, we recommend that you do the same thing these teams did: spend a half-hour or more reviewing the situation, then define high- and low-end brackets based on how realistically optimistic you are about resource allocation, and finally come to a mid-range figure that the whole team can endorse. Although there's no exact or right answer here, it's still important to aim for as much precision as possible, for the two reasons that we mentioned at the beginning of this chapter: A good Revenue Target quantifies the expected yield that you'll get from your Focus Investments, and it provides a business case for your executives—the account manager and those other senior people whose approval is going to be essential for the allocation of resources.

It isn't just those people, though, to whom you should bring the results of a Revenue Target exercise. You should also show it to your Field of Play. The experience of one LAMP client, a large Australian dairy producer, indicates why this can be an invaluable reality check as you're drafting projections.

For some years the dairy producer had been selling about $300 million annually to Coles, the continent's largest supermarket retailer. In a joint strategy session attended by the general and product managers from both companies, the dairy group team laid out fifteen or twenty Single Sales Objectives that they believed they could deliver in the next two years, getting very specific feedback—both positive and negative—on each one. Then, when it came to defining Revenue Targets, they told the Coles people that they hoped they would be able to do about $340 million with them in the coming year. After assessing the situation, the Coles people suggested that this figure was probably too conservative: "Based on the objectives and the investments we've discussed," said the supermarket general manager, "we ought to be able to give you more like $350 or $360 million." That was highly encouraging feedback that the dairy people would never have gotten unless they had discussed their revenue projections directly with the customer.

We reiterate here a principle that governs all of LAMP strategy. If you're truly partnering with your Large Account, then you don't play the cards that you're holding close to the vest. You share your plans for yourselves as well as for them. That's the only reliable way of improving mutuality, of checking whether they fully understand what you're doing for them—and what, in the name of fairness, you expect in return.

You do this, in the end, for the most practical of reasons: Without the Field of Play's approval, *no* Revenue Target—not even the most modest one—can honestly be considered a real-istic figure.

What About Quotas?

Setting Revenue Targets in the manner we've just described should lead to sensible and reliable forecasting. But we admit that in the real world, it doesn't always work this way. In the real world people who manage accounts have quotas. They probably don't like them, and they probably complain that those who set them have lost touch with what's happening in the trenches. They also probably *meet* them, with some regularity.

Given this reality, why bother with setting bracketed Revenue Targets? What's the virtue of a revenue-forecasting method that seems to ignore (if not confront) the field-tested stick-and-carrot quota system? There are several equally field-tested answers to these questions.

First, quotas are typically set at the regional, branch, or office level. What works, however fitfully, on these micro levels should not be expected to work with any consistency on the macro level of account management.

Second, quotas are by nature tactical, not strategic. Even the most strategically minded companies tend to look first at quarterly, and only later at annual, revenue in assessing how accounts are being managed. Focusing on a longer-term Revenue Target helps you put all the quarterly pieces of revenue in perspective; it provides a view of account growth (or shrinkage) that you're liable to miss when you're cranked up to make that last, essential sale by the end of July.

Third, the one-to-three-year Revenue Target provides a check on the realism of quotas. Quotas that are set without reference to such a strategically valid forecasting tool often turn out to be wild guesses.

Fourth, and perhaps most surprising, a strategically sound Revenue Target can actually provide greater incentive than the old meet-the-numbers routine. One of the great unsung lessons of the "productivity through people" programs of a few years back was that, when line salespeople were allowed to set their own quotas, they typically set them *higher* than their managers had. This suggests that the team-generated, long-term forecasts generated by bracketing Revenue Targets might provide more challenges to sales forces and Large Account management teams than the old, "top-down" imposed quota system.

The ultimate virtue of a Revenue Target that is generated collectively by a well-informed account team is that it provides a *realistic* picture of anticipated revenue. Since it's based on a detailed Situation Appraisal, and since it's reviewed and modified by the account's own Strategic Players, it substitutes rational discourse for wishful thinking and provides a shared, on-the-ground assessment of downstream potential that is by its very nature more reliable than even the most sophisticated mathematical model. That gives it a major advantage over mere quota setting.

It comes by that advantage honestly because, unlike a quota, a Revenue Target is a mutually agreed-upon description. Implicit here is the very difference between transaction-based selling and true account management. Quotas tell a sales team how much product their manager wants them to push. Revenue Targets define the quantifiable and reasonable benefits a supplier should realize when he delivers value to a company with whom he is partnering. There's all the difference in the world between those perspectives.

CHAPTER 15

Pre-Action Overview

"Have a care o' th' main chance,
And look before you ere you leap."

—Samuel Butler

ONCE YOUR TEAM HAS DEFINED ITS REVENUE TARGETS, YOU'VE COMpleted the analysis phase of your Large Account strategy, and you're ready to start assigning Actions that will make it operational. Before doing that, though, you'll probably find it useful to consolidate all the information you've gathered into a single, detailed summary of the account situation.

At the end of each two-day LAMP session, our clients typically spend a full hour doing this, so that they can produce a large, single-sheet Overview of where things stand. In this chapter, to give you a fuller sense of what such a summary exercise can accomplish, we present a checklist of last-minute clarifying questions as well as a sample filled-in Overview based on the PreComm case study.

Pulling It Together: A Final Checklist

Once you've reached this point in LAMP strategy, you've already asked yourselves dozens of clarifying questions. Here are just a few more, designed as last-minute double checks as you pull it all together.

The Buy-Sell Hierarchy. Is the position we've identified as our level on the hierarchy consistent with the customer's perception of our relationship? Is our planned movement to the next level—if that's where we want to be—realistic considering our current position?

Strategic Players. Does our Sponsor have authority and/or influence in this Field of Play? Does our Strategic Coach have credibility there? Do the key players from our organization align appropriately with those from the Field of Play?

Trends. Have we missed a Trend on the horizon whose emergence could affect the Field of Play's business environment?

Opportunities. Are the Opportunities we've identified really Opportunities for the Field of Play? If we help the Field of Play achieve them, will we reach our Goals?

Strengths. Do the Strengths we've identified clearly differentiate us from the competition? Does the Field of Play view them as Strengths? Will they help the Field of Play achieve the identified Opportunities?

Vulnerability. Is the Vulnerability we've identified the most significant Achilles' heel at the moment? Is it a weakness that we cannot afford to ignore?

Charter Statement. Does our Charter Statement clearly define the added value for the Field of Play? Would the Strategic Players recognize us from this statement? Are we comfortable sharing it with them?

Goals. If our Goals are met, will we be perceived as higher on the Buy-Sell Hierarchy? Do the Goals support the Charter Statement?

Focus Investment. Does the Field of Play perceive value in the Focus Investments we are planning to make? Do these investments focus effectively on the Field of Play's most significant Opportunities?

Stop Investment. Have we made the decision to make each Stop Investment in conjunction with the Field of Play? Have we determined whether each one is a temporary or a permanent Stop Investment?

Single Sales Objectives. If we close these sales, will they help us achieve our Goals? Will each close contribute to our Revenue Target? Are we pursuing any Single Sales Objective that does not contribute to our Goals?

Revenue Targets. Will the Single Sales Objectives listed help us meet this target? Are the Revenue Targets realistic given the identified time frame?

PreComm's Pre-Action Overview

To see an example of the team "deliverable" that the above exercise is designed to produce, here's the Pre-Action Overview that Pat Murphy and his PreComm team put together in their analysis of the Datavoc account.

Pre-Action Overview

Field of Play
- European Manufacturing division, Datavoc

Account Team
- Pat Murphy
- Sam Jones
- David Olsen
- Robert Glock
- Alicia Carvounis

Buy-Sell Hierarchy
- Now: Level 2
- Last year: Level 1
- Three years from now: Level 3 or 4

Strategic Players
- Sponsors: Pete Sanchez, Alan Coates
- Strategic Coach: Nick Constantinides
- Anti-Sponsor: Dave Kaufman

Trends
- Insurance costs due to liability claims.
- Competition from Asian imports and quick-to-market new products.
- Reduced margins on European manufactured products.

Opportunities
- Reduce production costs through Global Commodity Sourcing.
- Improve production and product launch times.
- Reduce cost of component failures and resulting liability.

Strengths
- Global reach enables us to source manufacture in least costly regions.
- Our design capability and understanding of technology are second to none.
- We deliver on time every time.

Vulnerabilities
- Our history of working successfully with their competition.
- Dave Kaufman's antipathy to Robert Glock.

Charter Statement

- Datavoc's European Manufacturing division will achieve a reduced time-to-market and enhanced consumer reputation by using our reliable, cost-effective components and VoIP technology. In return we will gain the major share of their overall spend in our market.

Goals

- Be seen by Alan Coates as the supplier on whom he could rely for components with good reliability and minimum DOAs (Level 2).
- Be acknowledged by procurement as the vendor with the best performance in terms of flexibility and just-in-time delivery (Level 3).
- Be acknowledged by Heather Rist to Dave Kaufman as the supplier that offers best whole-life component costs versus unit base price (Level 2).
- Be seen by Dave Kaufman as having done enough to reverse the damage done by our negation of the design agreement (eliminate Vulnerability).
- Be recommended by Pete Sanchez to Mark Duval as the expert design partner for the next family of Datavoc's air-conditioning controller units (Level 3).
- Be seen by Datavoc's European Manufacturing board as the supplier who helped them consistently control costs (Level 3 or 4).

Focus Investments

- Reestablish a mutually satisfactory design agreement.
- Become indispensable to their new product design process.
- Ensure that Datavoc will get timely, cost-effective delivery.
- Demonstrate our reliability with statistics.
- Demonstrate the impact of product failures on brand choice.
- Show that our "higher" unit cost actually translates into a lower lifetime cost of ownership.

Stop Investments

- Stop free design collaboration.
- Reassign smaller account.

Revenue Target

- $170 million annually over next three years.

"The Best Thing You Can Do"

We've often mentioned our conviction that, in setting Large Account strategy, one of the most valuable things you can do is to share that strategy, as it emerges, with the Field of Play. We'll end this section of the book by reiterating that point, and by referencing a fellow LAMP enthusiast whose experience underscores it.

Patrick Thomas is the Development Director for Global and Strategic Accounts at Aon, which manages insurance for giant corporations worldwide. When we asked him what he thought about sharing a Pre-Action Overview with a targeted Large Account, he admitted that, when he asks his account teams to do this, there's often initial resistance. "When you're showing your accounts such specific, personal Goals, and such concrete revenue projections," he says, "many account teams find it rather odd. It's like they don't want to disclose a secret plan. But once they go in and start sharing that information, it can really enhance your position.

"When you speak directly to an account like this, you often gain all kinds of inside information that you didn't have before. You learn about sponsors and relationships and buying process—all kinds of information that you need to be able to develop a commitment. That can have an incredible impact on strategy. When we offered to share one of these overviews with a major energy supplier, we ended up spending three hours with a senior executive. We showed him what we knew and what we didn't know—we actually pointed out the blank spaces on the sheet. He was fascinated by the whole process. He understood immediately that we were going out of our way not to waste his time. And he knew that it would help both of us enormously if we got the picture right."

Partly because of that strategy-sharing session, Aon did get it right, and—with the active help of the energy executive—significantly improved its relationship with his account. So, what had seemed to some on the Aon team as a radical move turned out to be the lever of a mutual Win. "Having the Large Account check your information can be a real gold mine," Thomas says. "As unusual as it strikes many people, in practical terms it's probably the best thing you can do."

PART IV

Execution

CHAPTER 16

Actioning the Strategy

"Actions speak louder than words."
—Traditional saying

ONCE YOU'VE GOT ALL YOUR INFORMATION AND PROJECTED STRATEGY development laid out neatly in an account management Overview, some obvious questions arise: How do we translate this blueprint into reality? What specific activities must we now put in place to move our companies' relationship forward and deliver on our Goals? Who should perform those activities, and on what schedule? In short, what steps must we take to move from strategic account analysis into action?

In our LAMP programs, account teams spend a full afternoon answering these questions, and coordinating the answers into a detailed Action Plan. In this chapter, we present the elements you need to develop such a plan, and we give examples of some essential activities that a good Action Plan includes. Those activities typically fall into one of the following four categories:

- Information gathering
- Sales and Support Programs
- Action items
- Reviews

Information Gathering

By the time you reach this point in a LAMP analysis, you've already done a great deal of gathering, collating, and discussing account information. In a sense, that's *all* you've done; you've pulled together the data you need in order to understand the account, and to set an appropriate strategy for improving your two companies' relationship. For this reason, it may seem redundant to suggest that, as you start to move from analysis to action, you take yet another crack at gathering information.

Based on long and often painful experience, though, we know that, however rigorous your information gathering has been, there is *always* something missing before you can move to action. We can't of course tell any individual account team what that something is—it varies depending on the situation. But we can say with confidence that failing to take a long hard look at your information—and the gaps in your information—at this point is often the difference between getting to your Goals and falling short. Once they've pulled everything together into an account Overview, successful teams always ask one more question: "Is there any information missing from this strategic analysis that, if we don't uncover it, may prove to be a liability?"

Account teams that are honest with themselves almost always find that the answer to that question is yes. And so the first step they take in "actioning the strategy" is to assign someone to secure each missing piece of data. When secured, the missing pieces may of course require a rethinking of the strategy overall. But not performing this pre-Action check can be disastrous.

Sales and Support Programs

The second type of "actioning" is to set up what we call Sales and Support Programs, which are the natural outgrowth of your Focus Investments. These programs, while they may in some cases support one or more of your Single Sales Objectives, are generally broader-based (and longer-term) initiatives that support account development overall—which of course can have a direct impact on your Revenue Targets. Sales and Support Programs often require the allocation of formerly unbudgeted resources, or the redirection of budgeted ones, to meet an emerging or urgent need in the Field of Play.

The computer hardware manufacturer Computer Lab, for example, counts Microsoft among its Large Accounts. A couple of years ago, to facilitate the delivery of their components to the software leader's many business units, Computer Lab opened a store on Microsoft's Redmond, Washington, campus. With this unusual support program, they simultaneously rationalized a complex shipping problem, demonstrated on-site commitment to the Large Account, and—not so coincidentally—made buying components from Computer Lab a whole lot easier.

Here's a second, personal example. We have one British client whose business with us expanded suddenly over the past three years. Some months ago, it became clear to us that, with more and more of their people using our services, they could probably use a dedicated support person in our London headquarters. So we selected a program-support person who knew the account and rewrote her job description so that, for a six-month period, she would devote 100 percent of her time to meeting this account's needs. This was a significant investment for us, but it paid off for everybody. The British firm appreciated the single point person, she was able gradually to train their people so that the dedicated contact was no longer necessary—and the support earned Miller Heiman a platinum-level reference.

These two examples merely hint at the range of activities that a company might want to introduce as Sales and Support Programs. Consider some other examples:

- Canvassing a division of a Large Account for new prospects.

- Generating leads through a direct mail campaign.
- Including in-product questionnaires to gauge customer satisfaction.
- Implementing an "executive call" program between managers in your Large Account and your company.
- Conducting needs surveys of current accounts.

In these particular examples, the emphasis seems more on sales than on support. But it's important not to overemphasize the distinction between those two words. In a sense, every good sales effort supports the customer, and every good customer-support system is likely to improve sales. So it makes a certain practical sense to consider them together—as two aspects of the same relationship-building endeavor. In fact, companies that implement "sales" programs like these often can't say precisely where the money will come from. When you send out thousands of customer reply cards, you don't know which returns will turn into real prospects. When you send your operations vice president to call on a Large Account's CEO, you're not aiming for just one piece of business. Such programs are meant to secure revenue growth over time, not to get approval for individual contracts.

Other programs may seem to favor support over sales, since they are even less directly connected to individual pieces of business. Consider the many backup and follow-up programs that companies initiate in order to ensure customer satisfaction, but that don't figure into anybody's quotas or commissions. For example:

- Customer-training programs
- Installation or upgrading of equipment
- Maintenance and "protective maintenance" service calls
- Repair calls
- Extended warranty programs
- Customer service 800 lines

In programs like these, the revenue payoff isn't always clear. They might be likened to operating feedback mechanisms designed to measure, and adjust, the existing revenue effort. They are usually implemented not by sales or account teams but by engineers, customer service people, or outside consultants. So their connection to revenue can sometimes seem distant. This does *not* mean that they're unimportant—or that they don't impact revenue positively. Again, the point is not to distinguish sharply between sales and support, but to understand them as complementary aspects of the same business endeavor. In the long run what both of them do is to help build relationships.

Sales and Support Programs strike some observers as peripheral to account management—as added cost items that aren't essential. That misreads their value. In a real sense, truly managing Large Accounts today *means* implementing Sales and Support Programs—including those that don't hook up to Single Sales Objectives. Such programs often provide the differentiation you need to elevate your position in the customer's mind from Level 2 to Level 3 on the Buy-Sell Hierarchy. *Not* implementing such programs means surrendering competitive advantage to the companies that do.

It's true that these programs put pressure on company resources. But thinking of this pressure as merely negative is strategically shortsighted. It's also, logistically speaking, not accurate. The planning and implementation of such programs doesn't necessarily mean *more* money or *more* work. It means the intelligent *reallocation* of funds and efforts so that you get better results.

For this reason, Sales and Support Programs should grow naturally out of Focus Investments. Focus Investments are the "what" that you need to implement to achieve your Goals; Sales and Support Programs are the "how"—the specific activities that must be put into place to realize the "what." For example, recall the Focus Investments made by the electronics company trying to assist a manufacturer's QC department:

- Provide them with better quality control process and measures.
- Help them focus better on how to sell to the Navy.

Specific Sales and Support Programs that would support those general initiatives might sound like this:

- Provide additional consulting in electronics testing to their QC control lab.
- Hire as a consultant a retired manager from the Large Account to understand better how they now sell to the Navy.

For another example, remember the Focus Investments that the PreComm team identified as being necessary for achieving their Goals:

- Reestablish a mutually satisfactory design agreement.
- Become integral to their new product design process.
- Ensure that Datavoc will get timely, cost-effective delivery.
- Demonstrate our reliability with statistics.
- Demonstrate the impact of product failures on brand choice.
- Show that our higher unit cost actually translates into a lower lifetime cost of ownership.

Those were the "what" items on a dedicated action agenda. To make those items operational, here are the Sales and Support Programs that Pat Murphy's team decided had to be put into place:

- Have Pat Murphy commit all his time and effort to managing the Datavoc account.
- Have the legal department devote time to setting up a new contractual framework for a design agreement.

- Assign a market researcher to acquire data on consumer trends that we can use to help Datavoc define future products.
- Have Robert Glock set up an internal transfer system to help ship our Chinese-manufactured components to Europe.
- Assign an administrative assistant to Pat Murphy to help track and manage Dead on Arrivals so we can prove our reliability with statistics.
- Carry out or acquire a consumer survey on product failures and impact on brand choice.
- Produce a financial report comparing unit costs to whole-life costs for the range of chips and ICs that Datavoc purchases from all suppliers (this will require Datavoc's agreement and involvement).

For each of these, you can see that the program supports the general intention of the Focus Investment by making it specific and accountable. To draft the new design arrangement, legal has to work on a contract; to prove reliability, a new assistant has to track DOAs; to prove the impact of product failure, PreComm needs to conduct a survey; and so on. Sales and Support Programs "hows" activate the Focus Investment "whats."

What Kinds of Programs?

Sales and Support Programs come in an almost infinite variety, depending on the specifics of Large Account situations. To help you identify programs that would be helpful to your relationships, your team may want to discuss the following five areas.

Area 1: Solving the customer's problems. Concentrate first on programs you might put into place that can address any of your Large Account's problems. The programs don't have to be related to individual sales; they don't even have to connect to the business you do with the account. For example, ask:

- What can we do to remedy a customer's *service* problem? Either our service to the customer, or its service to its customers.
- What can we do to solve a customer's *product* problems? Again, this means either the products we provide the customer, or those that it provides its customers.
- The last time we solved a problem for this customer, how did we do it? The last time our competition solved a problem for this customer, how did they do it?
- Is there a problem on this customer's horizon that a program of ours might head off? What activities might we engage in that could help us save the Large Account before it's in trouble?

Area 2: Addressing the customer's top-level issues. Now look at possible business results that you could provide to this Large Account. Remembering that long-term account management rests on satisfying top-management concerns, ask:

- What activities could we pursue to position us higher up the Buy-Sell Hierarchy?
- How can we help this account increase *sales revenue* from its own accounts?
- How can we improve the account's own *productivity*?
- Can we do something to help reduce its *costs*?
- What can we do to help this customer untangle an *internal* problem?
- What actions can we undertake that will have a positive impact on the customer's *profit*?

Area 3: Broadening your scope. Look at areas of potential activity that would broaden the scope of your "investment" in this Field of Play or this Large Account. Define programs that might target business you have overlooked. Ask:

- What sales and marketing approaches could we try that we haven't tried before?

- What are we doing with other accounts that we haven't considered doing here?
- Have we overlooked any Opportunities here? What programs would altering the Field of Play or our Charter Statement suggest?
- What other locations or business units of this Large Account have problems that we might address?

Area 4: Confronting threats. Think defensively for a few minutes. You may feel yourself to be on the offensive with this account at this time. But suppose you were being pushed into a corner. What extra effort would you then begin to consider? Ask:

- If our job(s) depended on a 50 percent increase in revenues this year from this account, what programs would we come up with?
- What actions might our major competitor take to unseat us in this account? Are any of those actions applicable to our situation? That is, do they suggest programs we could put in place?
- If we were about to lose the account, what defense would we take? If it was a choice of do or die, what would the extra effort be?

Area 5: Stretching the budget. To counter the all-too-common objection that the budget won't allow innovation, pretend there's no such thing as a budget. Ask:

- If a Fortune 500 company wanted to own this account, what programs would *it* put into place?
- What would we do with a blank-check program-development fund? In an ideal world, with no resource limitation, what activities would we pursue for this account?

We realize these final questions are "off the wall." But they're also useful in getting account teams to entertain innovation, to think beyond the old "resource-constrained" mentality that can limit options in the most hardworking of organizations. In fact, seldom does the simple lack of resources inhibit Support Programs. Usually the problem is that *too many resources are being devoted to dead-end, low-potential business.* Free up those resources by Stop Investment, and you'll be amazed at how many programs suddenly fall within budget.

Action Items

A third category of actioning activities is designed to concretely and specifically support the strategy elements that your team has worked with in the Situation Appraisal and analysis segments of the LAMP process—everything from your position on the Buy-Sell Hierarchy to the realization of your Revenue Target. An ideal Action would support all of these elements, but every reasonable Action must support at least one. You should also make sure that you assign at least one Action to mitigate the effect of every Red Flag—that is, elements in your analysis that you consider weak or uncertain. Depending on severity, such elements may require more than one Action.

Here's a personal example of actioning activities. One of our Large Accounts, a major energy company, wanted very fine-grained visibility into how the participants it was sending to our workshops were responding to its lessons. We agreed with our Sponsor there to set up a Support Program that would send the account monthly updates about its participants' experiences. To put that program into effect, we had to arrange for our workshop coordinator to evaluate participants' experience, assign an internal resource person to develop reports based on the evaluations, and schedule meetings between the Sponsor and the coordinator to review the reports. Those were all Actions for which Miller Heiman people took responsibility. In addition, our Sponsor in the account committed to identifying and arranging any follow-up training that the reports may have indicated were in order. In all of these cases, we defined clearly and collectively exactly what had to be accomplished, who should do it, and a time frame in which it had to be done.

To ensure that your actioning process is similarly pragmatic, we recommend that your team test each suggested Action by measuring it against the following questions:

- Which Strategic Player or Players will this Action impact positively? In what way will he or she be affected?
- Will this Action have a positive impact on how the Field of Play perceives a current or emerging Trend?
- Will this Action help them capitalize on an Opportunity? Which one, and how will it do so?
- Does this Action play from at least one of our strategic Strengths? If so, will it be clear to the Field of Play that this is so? If not, will the Action at least serve to offset our Vulnerability? Will that be clear to the Field of Play?
- Does this Action follow logically from one or more of our decisions about Focus Investment and Stop Investment?
- Will it serve to reinforce the perceived value of one or more of our Sales and Support Programs?
- Is it likely to further the realization of a Single Sales Objective? Can we quantify what it is likely to contribute to our Revenue Targets?

You may not be able to identify Actions that hit all these points. But the better an Action measures up against these questions, the more likely it is to help you achieve your Goals.

Be aware, too, that some of your Actions may require complementary or enabling Actions by individuals in your Large Account—individuals like our Sponsor in the example above. As you draft a list of Actions, your team should discuss which Strategic Players or other people in the account are the most appropriate to perform those Actions, and also which of your team members are best qualified to follow up and take responsibility for them being done.

Reviews

Account strategy can work only if *all* those affected by the strategy buy into its basic propositions. To ensure that your Action plan works the way you want it to, you need to have three distinct groups of people review your strategy and either sign off on it as it exists or recommend modifications. This should be done as soon as possible after your team drafts the Action agenda. One of the most common reasons that teams fail to bridge the gap between analysis and action is that they wait too long after putting together a strategy to share it with the key players who can make it or break it. We therefore recommend that, within *no more than two weeks* after you've decided on your strategy, you bring it for approval to the following people:

First, all the members of your *account team* itself. This is obvious enough, because they're the ones who devised the strategy. But this last pre-Action check is not always done. *Everyone* who works on an Action Plan should review and endorse the final version. Endorsement includes publicly and in writing acknowledging those Actions for which they have personal responsibility.

Second, your company's *senior management*. Again this seems obvious, but it's seldom done. Because Large Accounts are the driving force of your business, your top management has got to know how they're being handled. Ideally, your top managers should be working members of your Large Account management teams themselves. Failing that, their minimum commitment should be to read and approve your Action plan and the strategy it supports. If they can't, or won't, then you may be kidding yourself about getting the corporate support you'll need to make the plan work. That's a strong statement, we realize; the experience of hundreds of companies proves its validity.

Third, you need to get review and approval from the Strategic Players in your Field of Play—and, if necessary, from any other Large Account individuals who could influence your relationship. This type of review isn't obvious at all, and it's seldom done, but it's just as essential as getting your own management to buy in. We don't mean you should ask the account's decision makers to initial every one of your Focus Investments (although, as we've mentioned, they should agree to any Stop Investments). But they should understand in general terms what you're about, and specifically they should be able to endorse your Charter, your Goals, the Opportunities you want to help them with, and your Sales and Support Programs. If you don't have this kind of client buy-in, you're cutting yourself off from support that's just as critical as internal resource support.

If you're uncomfortable with this idea, it may be because the Goals you have set with this account are not as consistent with a Win-Win relationship as your team supposes, or because your current position with the account is weaker than you imagined. If that's the case, it's wise to reexamine your position to see if correcting the reasons for your discomfort would involve a redefinition of your Goals. Asking your Strategic Coach for input may be the least stressful and most helpful way to clarify the situation. But you must clarify it. When you are positioned well at an account, you should have *no hesitancy in sharing with the firm's decision makers the substance of your plans.*

The presentation of account plans to your Field of Play is not only an important feature of Win-Win business. It's also a good reality check against blue-sky thinking. If Strategic Players at your Large Account can't or won't acknowledge the *mutual* advantages of your Goals and programs, you cannot build a partnership upon them.

But that's a negative way of putting it. You can also see it positively. When your Large Account *does* buy into the Goals you've targeted, you begin to see each other as part of the same team. And the strategy runs that much more smoothly. It's as if you have a "companion general" across the field, providing you information you could not get on your own. Pragmatics again: You make the Large Account part of your planning process not because it's a "nice" thing to do, but because it makes for better business.

This is a micro version of a broader point we have made throughout the book. Good Large Account management isn't magic. It's based on the principle that, when people believe you have their interests as well as your own at heart, they'll fight to keep doing business with you. If they don't believe that, they'll run just as fast to avoid you.

Once you have the Action plan approved by these critical players, it will be time to actually perform the Actions that have been approved. As we've said, the strategy may entail dozens of different Actions, and some of them might take one to three years to come to fruition. That's too long to wait to start seeing at least some results—and waiting would subject you to the uncertainties of a volatile environment. That is why we recommend revisiting Action plans periodically, to see what things have changed and where the strategy needs adjustment. In fact, we recommend that you review and if necessary revise every Action plan no later than ninety days from the date of its inception. LAMP is decidedly a dynamic process, designed to respond as needed to constant change. This means that it requires frequent updating of your Actions. In the next chapter, we'll show you how to perform such an updating.

CHAPTER 17

Ninety-Day Review

*"In the business world, the rearview mirror is
always clearer than the windshield."*

—Warren Buffett

THE LAMP PROGRAMS THAT WE DELIVER FOR OUR CORPORATE CLIENTS
involve three distinct phases: a pre-program phase of fact gathering and account analysis, the program proper, and a ninety-
day follow-up workshop. The research that we described in
Chapter 5 corresponds to LAMP's pre-program phase. Parts II
and III of the book correspond to the program proper. We're
now going to introduce you to the review analysis that our
clients do in the follow-up workshop.

This third phase is not an add-on. It's a critical component
of LAMP strategy for the simple reason that the world is always changing. Any Action plan that you devise for a Large
Account depicts what you *intend* to have happen over the sub-
sequent twelve to thirty-six months. Any number of internal
and external imponderables could impact what actually *does*
happen. So running periodic rechecks of your strategy is indispensable. Only by frequent reassessment can your team keep
on top of what's happening in the account, quarter by quarter,
identify new Trends and Opportunities, and reallocate whatever resources are necessary for course correction.

As we've mentioned, we stipulate that the first major

reassessment of your position should come no later than the ninety-day mark, or one fiscal quarter into the strategy. We choose this checkpoint not arbitrarily, but based on decades of experience. After running upward of two thousand LAMP strategy sessions with corporate clients, we've found that on average it takes at least a couple of months for the planning done in those sessions to begin to bear fruit; yet, four or five months down the line, it may already be too late to make critical corrections.

In this chapter we outline a basic agenda for this Ninety-Day Review. The first step in setting up such a review, after deciding on a date, is to secure attendance commitment from everyone who needs to be there. That includes not only your account team members but also sales and general management in your company and key players in the targeted Large Account. Once that step is in place, here are some areas you should be looking at in your strategy reassessment.

Charter Statement

Every Charter Statement your team devises for a Large Account should identify four things: the Field of Play within the account, the value your company intends to bring to that Field of Play, the products or services that will bring them that value, and finally the return that your company will get from making this contribution. After ninety days, you should look carefully again at those four pieces. In the light of what has occurred since you agreed on the Charter, ask yourselves:

- Is this Field of Play still appropriate? Did we correctly define the scope of our operations in this account, and does that definition still apply? Have we been trying to reach too broad a portion of the targeted Large Account—trying to sell to too many people, departments, divisions, or other business units? Or, on the other hand, have we overlooked Opportunities that may benefit the Large Account by defining our Field of Play too narrowly?

• What value have we added, or are we currently adding, to this customer's business by focusing on this Field of Play? Are we providing solutions to the account's business problems, or are we still in a "cramming product" mode? Can we clearly define any business results that this customer has realized as a result of working with us? Are we comfortable with how we're now perceived by the Strategic Players, and are they fully aware of the contribution we're making?

• Are we delivering the *optimal* range of our products, services, or solutions? Not the broadest possible range, but the best one. Are our offerings proving to be too wide or too narrow for what this customer really needs? What products or services might we withdraw from consideration without sacrificing our effectiveness in the account? What products or services might we add?

• What benefit have we been receiving in return? If we're truly delivering value, what indication has the Field of Play given that they understand and appreciate that fact? Are they on record, either internally or publicly, as acknowledging our company's progress in building a relationship?

Once you've discussed these questions, decide as a team whether the Charter Statement you established three months ago still makes sense, or whether it has to be rewritten against today's reality.

Progress Points

In any ninety-day period, some things are going to go right and others wrong. In this step, define what's been going right: the major progress points of your Large Account strategy. Focus on three separate types of accomplishments:

• *Goals*. Note here any evidence you have that the Strategic Players in your Large Account are closer now than they were ninety days ago to perceiving your contributions in the way that you want them to be perceived. If you're successfully moving toward your Goals, you should be able to measure that progress in terms of the Field of Play's actual statements or actions.

- *Sales and Support Programs.* Write down those programs that you have successfully put in place, whether or not they have resulted yet in identifiable revenue. What specific *progress* do you see in the account for each of the programs that have been put into place? For programs that are still in the development stage, write down the progress that your team sees toward their implementation. Whether or not you've realized actual revenue from these programs, you can still be specific: "Karen Jensen made first executive call on their finance vice president." "Chicago direct mail campaign now in progress."

- *Revenue gains.* That is, individual Single Sales Objectives achieved (on or before schedule), or any other product or service packages placed with this Large Account. Define these precisely: "They bought the E19 calibrators we had planned to deliver" or "We placed twelve, rather than the anticipated ten, calibrators." For each sales "victory," note the revenue brought in and the close date. Compare these figures to the "intended" figures that you used to develop your Revenue Target. Are you on schedule in moving toward the objectives?

There may be other progress points that your team wants to note. You define them. In this regard we encourage you to be inclusive rather than limiting, provided that each identified accomplishment is clearly moving your account team ahead in its long-term strategy. Example: Taking an executive from the Large Account to lunch might well be a significant strategy accomplishment, but *only* if that person has significant influence with your Field of Play, and only if the results of that meeting included greater commitment from the client, and thus improved position for you.

Commitment must be mutual. It's never enough for a customer merely to "think about" the terms of a business relationship while the seller commits real time and resources into moving it forward. Yes, the seller may have to bear the weight at the outset, but if you're having trouble meeting with key players, or if you've met with them three times and they *say* they're interested in working with your company, but the only commitment you can get out of them is a vague "Let's talk again soon," you may be wasting each other's time. It may be time not for Focus but for Stop Investment.

Commitment means commitment to *concrete, scheduled actions*. These may range from merely setting up the next appointment to giving detailed responses to proposal specs to the actual signing of an agreement. But the customer must demonstrate interest by making incremental investments of *his or her* resources as the negotiating process between you moves forward. As you enter your Ninety-Day Review, use this understanding to check on your progress. What specifically has this customer done in the past ninety days to indicate an increasing level of interest in the relationship? What has it cost his or her company in terms of time and resources? If the investment is all on your side, it's not a partnership.

One good test of commitment is the extent to which the Large Account has expressly acknowledged the contribution you have made to its business. Whether internal or external, such acknowledgment is a critical measure of the return you're getting. If it hasn't been forthcoming within ninety days, your team may have to be more proactive in "merchandising" your contributions—making them crystal clear to the Strategic Players—so the Large Account not only understands what they are, but is willing to serve as a reference for your strategic Strengths.

Problem Areas

Now look at the things that have gone wrong, or failed to move forward rapidly enough, in the past ninety days. Investigate the following problem areas:

- *Revenue problems*. Look both at Single Sales Objectives that have been lost to the competition and at revenue opportunities that might have been developed in this Large Account, but that neither you nor your competition has capitalized on. For each piece of lost or undeveloped revenue, your team should identify *why* it was lost: "We're not well enough positioned with their operations people." "Our competition has a better service record." Discuss what changes might be made in your strategy to prevent similar losses in the future. Obviously the presence of Large Account people here can be especially valuable; no one will know better than they do why you lost a particular piece of their business.

• *Program and resources issues.* What internal program and resource issues must still be resolved in order to put your plan into operation? Are budget constraints impeding your progress? Do you have to do more aggressive internal selling to free up the funds needed to manage this account? How do your company's top managers view your proposed Actions? Are they committed to implementing them, or must they still be convinced that they're worth the investment? Could any of the revenue losses you've identified have been prevented by a fuller resource commitment?

• *Potential Stop Investments.* Since you laid out the Action plan, have there been any Focus Investments, Sales and Support Programs, or other significant resources allocated to this account that have proved irrelevant or contradictory to the strategy plan? Strategy by definition brings you closer to a sound long-term relationship. What activities have you been performing that aren't doing that? They may be candidates for a Stop Investment. If your team can identify any activities that aren't clearly bringing you closer to your Goals, write them down, explain *why* they're failing to live up to their promise, and consider dropping them from your Action plan. (Remember that Stop Investments must be discussed in advance with the Field of Play.)

• *Other obstacles.* What other obstacles stand in the way of an effective implementation of your Actions? List *anything* that has hindered your progress, no matter how trivial-seeming. Look especially for people in your own company or in the account who may lack full commitment to your plan, and areas where you lack information regarding the account and how its Strategic Players perceive your organization. Review the areas of account information that you addressed in the Situation Appraisal phase. Is the information you discovered there still valid? Any areas where you have unclear or incomplete information are by definition obstacles to an Action plan.

Reassessing Opportunities and Goals

In the Situation Appraisal section, we advised account teams to identify and concentrate on fulfilling their Large Account's three most significant Opportunities and, by doing so, to concentrate on meeting their own three most significant Goals. Ninety days out from a strategy session, it's time to revisit those choices, adjusting and redefining where necessary.

• For each of the Large Account's three best Opportunities, can you still define the *reason* it's important to the Field of Play? Has anything happened in the past ninety days to make you reconsider your initial evaluation? If an Opportunity is still seen by the customer as bringing value, your team should be able to explain why.

• Does each Opportunity still relate to your Goals? Look at each of the three Opportunities in turn. Can you identify *at least* one strategic Goal that the pursuit of this Opportunity will further? If not, should you drop this Opportunity in favor of another one? Or do your Goals themselves need redefining?

• Restate the three best Opportunities, based on the reassessment you've just performed and on changed conditions. They may be the same three you started out with three months ago, or you may have to redirect your actions and resources. Then do the same thing with your Goals. Consider whether they, too, may have to be redefined in the light of current reality.

• Finally, when you've reset the Opportunities and your Goals, review the list of Actions to which your team is committed. Does every Action contribute to the achievement of an Opportunity *and* a Goal? If not, it may be time to revise the list.

Revisiting the Action Plan

Once your team has thoroughly reviewed what progress has been made in the last ninety days—and what progress hasn't been made—you should be well equipped to revise your strategy. Almost certainly modifications will be in order. We suggest that you make changes to the plan not just by penciling in corrections on your original strategy statement, but by resetting the entire Action plan, so that it begins again, with today's date as the starting line.

If this sounds as if we're suggesting you rethink your Large Account strategy every quarter, you're right. In today's volatile markets, you must do this to retain any semblance of competitive advantage. It's only by periodically reviewing how far you've come, and making the necessary course corrections during every new review, that you can ensure your team is moving in the right direction—according to a Large Account management "map" that's up-to-date.

Perhaps the most critical feature of this resetting process is adjusting your Action schedule based on changing events and on the personal accountabilities that have (or have not) been established. After ninety days, some tasks are bound to have been done perfectly and some poorly or not at all. One of the most important benefits of regular review is to find out who's on board and who's asleep at the wheel—and to reappoint and reschedule team tasks accordingly.

For example, suppose during a LAMP analysis, one team member is assigned to present a contract for legal review by August 5. If the ninety-day review comes up on September 1 and that task hasn't yet been accomplished, you know that the entire Action plan has to be rescheduled, and the team has to understand the reason why the August 5 deadline was not met. This doesn't necessarily mean denouncing the accountable team member for negligence. He or she may have good reasons why the deadline wasn't met, and those reasons might provide information that will be useful to the realistic resetting of the schedule. But you won't *get* such information, in most cases, unless you ask—which is one reason that regular review is essential to strategy. Regular review *institutionalizes the asking of relevant questions*, so that nobody on your team has to labor under the delusion that Piece 14 of the strategy is working when it's not.

Regular review also provides *documented feedback* on where a plan is working effectively and where it's not. Most so-called account plans don't even try to do that: They're collections of old statistics and yesterday's news. A dynamic, constantly reassessed Action plan lets you know *while you can still do something about it* where it's working and where it needs retooling.

The purpose of a good Action plan isn't to predict with perfect accuracy where you and the Large Account will be in three years, or three quarters, or three weeks. It's to get agreement from your two companies on where you'd like the relationship to be after a reasonable amount of time, given continued commitment to mutual success. Even if that commitment remains rock-solid, between now and a few years from now any number of changes could take place that might force you to reconsider the shape of the relationship. That's why it's logical to constantly monitor the situation, adjusting when necessary to ensure continued value for the customer. Failing to do this risks delivering the message that your relationship with the Large Account can be taken for granted. Delivering that message, however unintentionally, is about the quickest way we know to lose a competitive advantage.

CHAPTER 18

The LAMP Advantage

"We've got to stop thinking beyond our guns.
Those days are closing fast."
—Pike Bishop in *The Wild Bunch*

IN DISCUSSING THE CURRENT LANDSCAPE OF ACCOUNT MANAGEMENT, we noted that, in many leading firms, the teams responsible for managing Large Accounts function not exclusively as sales or marketing entities but as semi-autonomous business units. They have their own, independent reporting structures, their own P&L responsibilities, and they are often headed by executive-level account managers with the authority to marshal whatever resources are needed to meet the rapidly changing needs of their "external assets."

Given the growing relevance of this model, at least among the most successful enterprises, perhaps it makes sense to think of Large Accounts today less as individual customers than as "markets of one." Certainly if they are judged by their behavior—by the way they respond to marketing and relationship-building overtures—they often behave as if they were complex markets rather than individual businesses. That is, they display all the volatility, responsiveness to global trends, and hunger for growth that financial and industrial markets tend to do, and they insist, as Adam Smith might have predicted, on rewarding only those overtures that provide them value. Any account management team intending to weather the competitive storms of today's economy must begin by recognizing this reality.

In the old days of account management—when large business customers were still considered chiefly sources of revenue—it was possible to go head to head with competitors based on product specs, and the company that offered the "best product at a fair price" often garnered the greatest wallet share of a given account's business. In the era of accounts as markets of one, this strategy is doomed. The only businesses that have a chance of sustaining competitive advantage today understand that it is relationships, not revenue per se, that provide the key to survival. They also understand that in building relationships, value *as perceived by the account* is the only kind that counts.

To deliver that kind of value, you need more than a good product, or good service, or even avid, sustained attention to the Large Account's needs. Above all you need the ability to track the changing business requirements of each market of one, and then to marshal whatever corporate resources you have at your disposal to address those needs *as only your company can.* Leveraging your unique strategic Strengths in this way is the secret to competitive advantage today, as has been demonstrated time and again in hundreds of alliances. Companies that serve their allies' business needs well prosper. Those that don't, fail.

But *how* to provide such service—that's the difficulty. And it's the difficulty for which the process we've described in this book provides a uniquely practical solution.

As we've explained, in order to serve your business partners well, and thus to maximize the mutual benefit of those "external assets," you must first fully understand their business situations; to do that, you use the sub-process we call Situation Appraisal. Next, you must perform a rigorous, team-based assessment of all the key elements that are affecting your relationship now, or might possibly affect it in the future; this is what we discuss as strategic analysis. Then you outline, in detail and with appropriate schedules, what initiatives will best enable the Large Account to maximize its Opportunities; which of your corporate resources should be leveraged against these initiatives; and how you will measure the success of these initiatives for both your companies. This is the Execution phase of a good Large Account strategy.

It's a tall order. It requires not only the formation of the right team—the right "business unit"—and the proper alignment of its people with the Large Account's key players, but also a firm commitment, throughout all levels of your organization, to the importance of building relationships with your markets of one, and a willingness to apply the resources that those relationships need. In an economy where managers are judged principally on quarterly sales reports, many companies are unwilling to make such a commitment. But in today's intensively competitive economy, with even your most "loyal" customers pushing you toward commodity, this unwillingness is tantamount to corporate suicide.

Current revenue is important, and it always will be. But the new way to grow account revenue isn't to push more product— or to train your biggest guns always on the most immediately lucrative deals. If you're not willing to bet on future revenue by growing your relationships—by thinking beyond your guns— your company, sooner or later, will be pushed off the Buy-Sell Hierarchy. And replaced by a competitor with a broader, more long-term vision.

The good news is that, for companies with that broader vision and that commitment to the future, the opportunities for getting back to growth have never been better. Precisely because many firms see nurturing their Large Account relationships as daunting, the field is open to those who welcome the challenge. In this book, we've tried to show that, with the appropriate process-oriented approach, managing a

Large Account, while never easy, is as feasible a corporate endeavor as it is necessary. We encourage you to accept the challenge of that endeavor, and to join the growing number of leading enterprises who are appreciating the manifold benefits of the LAMP advantage.

Your Customers Are Your Future: A Case for Strategic Account Management

Lisa Napolitano,
President and CEO,
Strategic Account Management Association

IN THE MIDST OF RAMPANT CONSOLIDATION AND RAPID GLOBALIZATION, customers are demanding far more from their suppliers than ever before as they rethink their business strategies to provide higher shareholder returns. For many organizations, a key component of strategy is to develop a laser-beam focus on their core competencies and outsource the rest. Part of the process includes sizing up suppliers to determine which ones can best help further their goals and rearranging their internal processes to concentrate on core relationships with these firms. By aligning themselves with fewer suppliers, customers hope to achieve greater accountability for results, greater financial transparency, and greater efficiency. In short, they want greater control.

To achieve such results, customers expect core suppliers to demonstrate the ability to:

- Impact their business performance across a range of products and geographies.

- Sustain the financial and competitive strength that signi-
fies long-term health of the firm.
- Invest in developing a unique set of services for the
customer.
- View the customer as strategically important.
- Make a sustained commitment to market leadership in
specific products and markets.
- Consistently deliver integrated service across the supplier's organization.

Taken together, these requirements change the ground rules
for achieving competitive advantage—indeed, for surviving in
the global economy. As customers choose among competing
suppliers, they are, in effect, determining your strategy. The
goal is not merely being selected, but deliberately aligning
with the marketplace winners of the future. Customers who
gain market share will take their core suppliers with them as
they prosper. Investing resources in marketplace losers, or allowing the competition to align with the winners, does not
bode well for your firm's future.

Strategic Customers As Assets

Proper customer selection is undoubtedly the underpinning
of successful strategic account management—doing all the
right things with all the wrong people is not a recipe for success. Too often, short-term focus or internal politics dictate
which customers get the label of "key/major/strategic/global/
corporate/alliance" account. With this approach, many turn
out to be future marketplace losers.

But even as suppliers apply more rigorous criteria for selecting strategic customers, they nearly always pick too many and
rarely employ an ROI analysis that an asset portfolio warrants.
Spreading resources too evenly across too many customers
practically guarantees the inability to add significant value to
the customer that you can get paid for. Such overextension re-

sults in a commodity mentality from customers and a coverage model too expensive to justify.

Customers who are marketplace winners don't just buy products and services, they buy expectations. What they want is problem solving and creative thinking about their business, which requires the commitment of and access to the supplier's total operation. To deliver on these expectations takes the efforts of your entire organization, which is precisely why it is *not* just about selling.

Selecting a sub-optimal customer portfolio is a common form of misalignment, as illustrated by a recent Strategic Account Management Association survey of three hundred sales executives from Fortune 1000 firms. When asked to evaluate their strategic customer portfolio, half said that less than one-third of their firm's key customers were likely to be long-term winners. Even more discouraging, a third said that between 50 and 75 percent of key customers have "uncertain" futures or are "long-term losers."

Clearly, the state of the typical customer portfolio indicates firms are a long way from truly viewing customers as assets. To do so requires boardroom involvement, enterprise-wide changes, long-term thinking, investment of resources, and a belief in the concept of relationship capital. Even firms held up as benchmarks in strategic account management are having difficulty adapting appropriately to these changes. Building an integrated view of the total customer relationship across products and geographies and leveraging your position around the world as one unit are enormous challenges under even the most favorable circumstances. Add to that a challenging economy characterized by cost cutting and short-term focus, and it's no surprise that even relationship-conscious firms struggle with investing the resources required to meet the growing business requirements of their most important customers.

Alignment: The Challenge of Strategic Account Management Execution

In their recent best-seller, *Execution: The Discipline of Getting Things Done*, Larry Bossidy and Ram Charan argue that execution is actually a discipline and a system that must be built into a company's strategy, its goals, and its culture. Without an execution culture, the perfect strategy is nothing more than a dream—some might even argue a nightmare. Senior executives routinely affirm that it is not the lack of a strategy that causes them to lose sleep, but, rather, their organization's inability to execute against a strategy, often long after they think they have expressed that strategy with near-perfect clarity. Their nervousness is understandable. *Fortune* magazine estimated recently that about 70 percent of failed CEOs were brought down by a failure to execute, not by flawed strategic thinking.

Why is it so difficult to execute? Often, the answer lies embedded in the company's organizational model. The execution of strategy in today's larger, more complicated organizations requires alignment across a myriad of functional, geographical, and product-focused silos. Yet alignment is tough to achieve in an environment where thousands of decisions and trade-offs must be made every day by individuals who have access to different information and have different—sometimes conflicting—objectives, responsibilities, and levels of accountability. Failure to align broadly and deeply around core strategies results in thousands of sub-optimal decisions that, though individually small, have a collectively huge impact.

This is especially true in the arena of strategic customer management, possibly the toughest execution challenge facing companies today. Why? Because the degree of alignment necessary to bring the collective value of your firm to bear on your customer's business is enormous. Effective SAM requires:

1. Securing the involvement and cooperation of multiple functional areas within both supplier and customer firms.

2. Integrating the different stakeholders into a single organization with a common identity and purpose.
3. Bringing the voice of the customer into your organization and mobilizing company-wide resources to focus on that voice.

What these three related requirements add up to is the need for an *enterprise* response to strategic customer needs. Yet sales organizations, externally focused by nature, have often found themselves paralyzed by customer expectations that require such a response. In their attempt to successfully mobilize their firm's resources and people, account managers and their teams often run head-on into apathy, contending priorities, and even active resistance. This is precisely where attempts to develop core relationships break down, because all the work trying to penetrate the customer to identify sources of new value is fruitless if the supplier can't or won't deliver on it.

There is no doubt that the need to achieve internal alignment is acute. One indication of this fact is that, while large customers are demanding a single point of contact for purchasing a company's products and services, field sales reps from the same firm are invading their offices to pitch the same business. Successfully implementing a more integrated mind-set requires understanding and buy-in from all stakeholders who have an impact on the customer. Yet, companies often underestimate the difficulties of achieving such internal alignment and fail to understand how the very structure of their companies works against it.

Getting Beyond the Silo Mentality

According to our research, the single biggest obstacle to alignment is a silo mentality that divides an organization into competing turfs. Because turf conflicts can surface in business units, functions, or geographies—and in many cases all three simultaneously—they are particularly insidious when you are trying to present one face to the customer. At the heart of such conflict are the simple realities of organizational structure and basic human nature, which is why the problem is so pervasive. Cooperation between entities is usually predicated upon clearly demonstrated benefits that do not simultaneously undermine the goals of the silo to which they are fundamentally loyal. If an entity perceives a threat to its authority, goals, or relationships—its power—it will often respond defensively in order to protect its turf.

The specific origins of turf battles are numerous and important to correctly diagnose in order to successfully defuse them.

- *Resources:* In a climate of shrinking resources, entities must compete for a piece of the pie. If one organization perceives the cost of cooperation in terms of money, time, or energy to be greater than the benefits, it will resist cooperating.
- *Goals:* Even if there is consensus on overarching corporate goals, specific joint actions can still be perceived as working against the overall interests of given segments of the organization or as impeding the achievement of departmental, functional, or individual goals.
- *Geography:* To allow another entity to operate in one's own geographical area is often perceived as an indication that the territory "owner" is not doing an adequate job. Sharing geographical territory may also be perceived as a duplication of effort or a source of potential confusion to target audiences.
- *Methods:* Despite general agreement on goals, conflict can still arise if one party feels the approach proposed to reach those goals would be ineffective or counterproductive to other interests of the organization. In addition, one organization, feeling ownership of a specific activity or technique, may be reluctant to have another organization adopt "its" method.
- *Identity:* Resistance may also occur when an organization feels that proposed cooperation would adversely affect how it is viewed by other entities both inside and outside the company.
- *Personalities:* Key players who are personally disliked by other stakeholders because they are perceived to represent a

political or organizational threat can undermine efforts toward collaboration.

Orchestrating an enterprise response to strategic customers requires the active participation of your various silos—and accepting the fact that these silos will always be present. Corporations of any significant size cannot make all the necessary transactional decisions "with one mind." To provide manageable spans of control and to benefit from functional specialization, companies are forced to subdivide their organizations into the very model that fosters misalignment. The key to moving beyond the silo mentality is to minimize the ensuing conflicts by acknowledging and understanding their origin and proactively fostering collaboration. This task is the primary work of the strategic account management program, whose primary role is to advocate for the customer across all parts of the firm. Because this challenge is universal, even incremental improvement in such alignment is a powerful source of competitive advantage.

The Role of the Executive Suite in Enabling Alignment

Minimizing turf issues is one key ingredient in SAM programs that work in practice, not just on paper. Another is senior management support, often itself a critical factor in overcoming the silo mentality. Our research shows that an overwhelming number of practitioners stress the importance of a SAM program being mandated from the top to truly achieve results. It's easy to understand why. Without executive support, it's difficult to get approval for ideas that require reallocating business units' revenue or spending capital dollars. A CEO who plays an active, visible role regarding SAM initiatives sends a strong message throughout the company regarding their importance, which helps establish the credibility and authority of the program. On the other hand, when senior management makes decisions or exhibits behavior counter to the SAM strategy, the results can be disastrous.

The executive suite can either put rewards in place to drive customer focus across the firm, or it can take the inverse approach and penalize those who don't comply. But one or the other has to be in place, or the account manager will end up spending more time putting out fires related to inconsistencies in strategy than in actually setting and implementing strategy with the customer.

In the best-case scenario, the sales organization leverages the power of the executive suite on an ongoing basis rather than only in dramatic, high-profile situations with gigantic stakes. When there are conflicting agendas, systems and policies are not always enough to prevent a stalemate in terms of handling a customer issue. It can take the sweeping authority of C level players to remove certain obstacles. The key here is to adopt a formal escalation process to respond quickly, decisively, and proactively.

Perhaps the greatest role the executive suite can play is direct contact with the customer itself. Strategic account managers can be more effective at selling to the executive level with the participation of their own executives, especially when they find themselves politically blocked by someone in the customer's organization. Moreover, when the executive suite is used in a focused way with strategic customers, it typically generates increased customer commitment and strategic-level conversations.

Creating Value Through Shared Knowledge

In the knowledge economy, the work of management is the creation of an intelligent organization—one that is nimble, creative, fast, and innovative in leveraging its intellectual capital to add value to the customer. CEOs today are heeding the advice of management guru Peter Senge, who wrote in his groundbreaking book, *The Fifth Discipline*, "The only source of competitive advantage in the future will be the knowledge that an organization contains and an organization's ability to learn faster than the competition." Alert to this fact, CEOs are increasingly focusing on knowledge management as a critical organizational competency. In a recent study, four hundred CEOs were asked to name the most important trends affecting their management decisions today. Eighty-eight percent of them identified knowledge management, second only to globalization, and ahead of traditional concerns such as cost reduction and supply chain management.

Why are CEOs so concerned about knowledge management? Because effective knowledge management helps you add value to the customer in a variety of ways. It can enhance overall business performance by eliminating redundancies, increasing quality and productivity, increasing customer responsiveness, and improving decision making. It can also fuel innovation by enabling all employees to contribute ideas and by systematically leveraging intellectual capital company-wide. It can even foster internal collaboration, which decreases competition among stakeholders inside an organization and gets everyone pulling in the same direction—that of the customer. Such a culture of collaboration can be a powerful tool for creating a similar climate with a firm's most important customers.

Yet herein lies another alignment challenge. Effective knowledge management is a cultural pursuit, not a technical one. Unfortunately, too many companies fail to understand that organizations leverage knowledge through networks of people who collaborate—not through networks of technology that interconnect. True value creation depends upon access not only to the right information at the right time, but to a culture of collaboration inside the firm. The IT graveyard is littered with companies that followed high-budget, "visionary" CIOs down the path of this or that client-server investment or new e-mail system, only to find that people still didn't want to collaborate to share and develop new knowledge. Bottom line: Interconnectivity begins with people who want to connect. After that, tools and technology can make the connection.

The truth is that people are competitive by nature and have a tendency to guard, rather than share, what they know. We think that what we know is what continues to provide us with long-term employment. A successful knowledge-management program requires changing that assumption and replacing it with an understanding of the "network effect"—an IT rule which says that the more information is shared (networked) the more powerful it becomes. In an internally aligned organization, executing a knowledge-based strategy is not about managing knowledge per se; it's about nurturing people with knowledge so they see that empowering their colleagues also empowers them.

People will not willingly share information with co-workers if their workplace culture does not support learning, cooperation, and openness. But because knowledge sharing does not occur naturally, it must be managed, encouraged, and rewarded. Employees must be induced to make "deposits" into whatever knowledge repository your company supports, either through reward or through punishment.

Employees must also understand what the knowledge is *for*. This means that, in developing an aligned, knowledge-based culture, sales leaders must make an explicit connection between their company's competitive strategy and how knowledge supports it. The new form of intellectual capital that Senge and others have rightly praised is meaningless from a business standpoint unless it helps to drive the old-fashioned objectives of serving customers better and beating competitors. If a company does not have its fundamentals in place, all the corporate learning, information technology, and knowledge databases are merely costly diversions. The old truth is still the best truth: A company has to know the kind of value it intends to provide and to whom. Only then can it link its knowledge resources in ways that make a difference.

Enter the Entrepreneur

In today's selling environment, account managers are being asked to manage all customer interactions and ensure that the entire team is providing high-quality responses and content on time—while at the same time being asked to play a strategic role in devising ways to sell deeper and wider into the account. Unfortunately, today's intricate corporate web of structures and relationships has created huge issues of coordination, consistency, and responsiveness. AMR Research has found that approximately 40 percent of most account teams' time is spent on day-to-day team coordination activities, not on strategic selling.

With strategic or global account managers, it's even worse. They struggle with how to drive increased results in a shorter time frame and at a lower cost. This is virtually impossible when, according to a recent SAMA study, team coordination responsibilities leave the average account manager only 11 percent of his or her time for sales activities, and only 25 percent for *all* customer-facing activities.

What is clear is that the account manager models that have prevailed for the past decade are no longer adequate to meet the needs of a firm's most important customers. The emerging role requires more than any organizational design can enable and more than any amount of personal motivation can possibly muster. That role, as SAMA data consistently indicate, more and more resembles that of an entrepreneur. The emergence of this role poses an additional, and as yet little understood, challenge to alignment.

The fact is that managing an existing customer relationship and developing strategic business within that relationship are related but distinct activities that require different skills, mind-sets, and types of focus. Too few firms understand this distinction or allocate sufficient resources to cover these two important areas equally effectively. Most are still lagging behind in creating what management guru Gary Hamel calls a "hierarchy of imagination." Intent for the past decade on "optimizing" operations—including account management—firms must now, asserts Hamel, focus more on "innovating" and creating customer value. This requires an entrepreneurial approach to managing strategic customers that has not yet been integrated into many sales organizations.

What's needed, suggests Dr. Kevin Wilson of the Sales

Research Trust, is the development of a "political entrepreneur" role like that of today's leading global account managers. His studies have shown that GAMs, who typically manage the most complex customers, are essentially concerned with identifying and exploiting opportunity, with solving problems that add value to the relationship, and with innovation in its broadest sense—all characteristics of the entrepreneur.

These characteristics are not common to most strategic account managers today. In fact, they are not common *human* characteristics, and are rarely the product of sheer intelligence, hard work, or training. The entrepreneur sees things that other people do not and acts upon those insights in order to create new value. Moreover, there are challenges that arise when dealing with truly entrepreneurial people. Research shows that most entrepreneurs start several businesses due to the fact that they always have great new business ideas flowing through their heads, but rarely stick around and actually run a company past the start-up phase because that role does not appeal to them. For this reason, entrepreneurs are not particularly well suited for the operational management of a supplier-customer relationship.

The important point is that relationship-oriented companies need *both* types of managers: those who excel at managing the day-to-day mechanics of the relationships and those with the capability to innovate. Firms must recognize this distinction in order to attract, deploy, and retain the right people who can collectively transform the way they do business with strategic customers.

The Customer-Centric Mandate

The reality in today's global corporate village is that it's a customer's world. The competition is fierce out there, and as progressive companies have found, the best way to retain customers is to become an actual extension of their customers. The name of the game, therefore, is customer-centricity. Anything less won't work in today's business environment.

How do you define customer-centric? At the Strategic Account Management Association, we've been able to get a broad, bird's-eye view of many companies' SAM programs, across numerous industries and around the world. Because each program is unique to the culture, industry, and market environment in which it operates, it's difficult to formulate prescriptions for customer-centric success. However, three patterns emerge, all relating to alignment, when we examine those SAM programs that are actually working for the customer:

1. *Executive commitment to customer-centricity*: A company's senior management must embrace the concept of customer-centricity as a driver of competitive advantage. The most successful strategic account management programs are truly an extension of the overall corporate strategy.

2. *Customer-centric account management*: In the elite SAM programs, strategic account managers know the customer intimately and act as customer advocates inside their own organizations. They are both willing and able to engage their organization's resources to bring value to the customer.

3. *Customer-centric organizational culture*: It takes the efforts of an entire organization to enable a supplier to deliver customer value. In effective SAM programs, cross-functional commitment is achieved through adequate incentive programs, constant communication, and a culture that reinforces the value of the strategy to all internal stakeholders.

There is distinct competitive advantage that will accrue to firms who, by institutionalizing these critical elements, can align better around their strategic customers to create real value. In the final analysis, it is only this degree of alignment that can effectively power your relationships with strategic customers. Customer-centricity is a mind-set you can't afford *not* to have.

Strategic Account Management Association
150 N. Wacker Drive, Suite 2222
Chicago, IL 60606
Tel: 312-251-3131   Fax: 312-251-3132
www.strategicaccounts.org

The Strategic Account Management Association (SAMA) is a nonprofit organization devoted to advancing and promoting the concept of customer-supplier collaboration. SAMA is dedicated to increasing the professional skills and knowledge of the individuals involved in the process of managing national, global, and strategic customer relationships, and to enabling firms to create greater customer value and achieve competitive advantage accordingly. Founded in 1964 and with nearly three thousand members worldwide, SAMA attracts the profession's most influential decision makers through its reputation as the knowledge leader in managing customers on an enterprise level. Members receive access to comprehensive trend and research data, global best practices, educational events, networking opportunities, and other tools needed to succeed.

INDEX

Robert B. Miller

Robert B. Miller brings almost forty years of experience in sales, consulting, and executive management to help clients succeed in the sales arena. As a recognized expert in complex sales management, he is the co-author of three best-selling business books—*Strategic Selling* (1985), *Conceptual Selling* (1987), and *Successful Large Account Management* (1991)—which have been translated into seven languages. He is also the co-author of a fourth book, *The 5 Paths to Persuasion,* published in 2004. He has built and managed several sales forces at national and international levels.

In the early 1970s Miller developed the *Strategic Selling* programs that he later incorporated into Miller Heiman, Inc. Prior to Miller Heiman, Mr. Miller was Vice President and General Manager of North American Operations for Kepner-Tregoe, Inc., a strategic consulting organization based in Princeton, New Jersey.

Stephen E. Heiman

Stephen E. Heiman rose in nineteen years from the level of National Account Salesman for IBM (where he increased sales in all product areas by more than 35 percent and was in the top 5 percent for total sales and percentage quota) to Director of Marketing at Kepner-Tregoe, to Executive Vice President of North American Van Lines. There he operated as General Manager of the $150 million Household Goods Division and, with full P&L responsibility, increased sales and profits by 36 percent in four years' time. In 1978 he joined Robert Miller as co-principal and full partner in what became Miller Heiman, Inc.

Tad Tuleja

The author of thirty-two books, Tad Tuleja has been associated with Miller Heiman since 1985, when he collaborated on its first best-seller, *Strategic Selling*. Since then he has written three other Miller Heiman books, edited the company newsletter, *Bestfew*, and—from 1997 to 2003—worked in marketing communications at Siebel Systems. Educated at Yale, Cornell, Sussex, and the University of Texas—from which he holds a Ph.D. in anthropology—Tuleja directed the University of Massachusetts School of Management writing program for four years. He has also taught at Baylor, Willamette, Colby, and Harvard, which awarded him a Certificate of Distinction in teaching. He currently teaches expository writing at the University of Oklahoma.

MILLER HEIMAN, INC. IS A GLOBAL LEADER IN BUILDING EXCEPTIONAL sales organizations. The company's team of world-class sales consultants helps organizations dramatically improve sales productivity through consistent, field-ready processes, benchmarking tools, development programs, and process consulting.

Best known for its time-tested *Strategic Selling®* program, Miller Heiman provides solutions for introducing a consistent sales process throughout an organization, identifying the strengths and weaknesses inherent in every sales force, and ensuring the cultural indoctrination of training programs.

With a prestigious client list including KLA-Tencor, BAX Global, Marriott Corporation, Dow Chemical, Pricewaterhouse-Coopers, and Wells Fargo, Miller Heiman understands the issues and challenges facing sales leaders in virtually every major industry, from manufacturing and consumer goods to technology and finance.

Prepare Your Entire Organization

The Miller Heiman portfolio of sales training and development services addresses the most critical aspects of the selling cycle. From getting the right people doing the right things to uncovering new opportunities with your most established accounts, we prepare your entire sales organization to succeed.

Our consulting and training is supported worldwide through a global network of more than two hundred sales consultants in over twenty-five countries. Each is an independent sales professional with an average of eighteen years of real-world sales and sales management experience. Prior to working with Miller Heiman, our sales consultants were sales directors and vice presidents, so they truly understand your challenges and aspirations.

Training Solutions

Our training solutions are proven to help establish and grow more productive customer relationships. These practical solutions include:

- *Conceptual Selling®*
- *Strategic Selling®*
- *Large Account Management Process (LAMP®)*
- *Negotiate Success^SM*
- *Channel Partner Management^SM*
- *Executive Impact^SM*

Benchmarking Tools

Our benchmarking tools can help you quickly evaluate the strengths and weaknesses of your sales organization, analyze personnel data against position requirements, and make sure you have the right people in the right positions. We help you establish benchmarks to reach your sales goals. We bring clarity to what works and what doesn't. These powerful tools include:

- *Predictive Sales Performance^SM*
- *StartPoint^SM*
- *Conversion, Penetration, Retention (CPR^SM)*

Sales Workshops

Throughout the world, we conduct hundreds of convenient and accessible sales workshops where your staff can learn the Miller Heiman sales process and apply it to real sales opportunities in their funnels. They'll learn to uncover why the customer is really buying, to identify a fit, and to develop and execute an action plan that's right for you and your customer.

For further information on LAMP or any of our other service offerings, call Miller Heiman today and we'll find you the right consulting partner who understands you, your company, and your market.

Miller Heiman Corporate Headquarters
10509 Professional Circle, Suite 100
Reno, Nevada 89521
1-877-552-1757
www.millerheiman.com

Miller Heiman International Headquarters
Nelson House, 1 Auckland Park
Milton Keynes, MK1 1BU England
+44 1908.211212
www.millerheiman.co.uk